Arthur: An Actuarial Odyssey

DM Baronov

Copyright © 2024 DM Baronov

All rights reserved.

ISBN: 9798335481236

Dedication

To Chien-ngo, whose life was stolen in the cruelest of fashions and who I miss very deeply

CONTENTS

Chapter One	1
Chapter Two	7
Chapter Three	16
Chapter Four	24
Chapter Five	41
Chapter Six	46
Chapter Seven	70
Chapter Eight	81
Chapter Nine	94
Chapter Ten	114
Chapter Eleven	134
Chapter Twelve	145
Chapter Thirteen	159
Chapter Fourteen	183
Chapter Fifteen	204
Chapter Sixteen	220
Chapter Seventeen	242
Chapter Eighteen	259
About the Author	273

Arthur: An Actuarial Odyssey

Chapter One

Arthur threw open the second floor bay window. Searching the yard, he called out into the night.

"Hark, who goes there? I beseech thee! Announce thyself as friend or foe!"

The thick night air hung still. In the shadows below a stranger scampered along the unlit garden path. Just then, a voice cried out in shrill tones.

"Uh... pizza man! Half pepperoni, half green pepper!"

Arthur turned to his guests.

"I am beckoned to the gate. Do forgive my briefly taking leave."

Arthur flew to the gate. Money and pasta were exchanged and he returned.

In the cold air, the light striking him as he coolly crossed the room, Arthur's pizza looked good—real good.

Arthur: An Actuarial Odyssey

His guests could not pull their gaze from it. They desired Arthur's pizza as they had no other before. With their stares they devoured Arthur's pizza. Arthur's coarse, manly hands ripped open the pizza box—exposing the white, virgin cheese dripping over the flaming pizza's offerings. His guests moved in on Arthur's pizza like a fresh kill. There it lay... naked... hot... inviting. No one asked for plates. They'd swallow this prey flesh and all—shameless in their savagery, hands drenched in blood-red, still warm sauce, mouths biting hard and deep into Arthur's pizza and all its sensuous toppings.

Arthur moved to the window. He saw below the bright moon's reflection on a dead cat in the alley way.

"A car crashes!" Arthur impatiently shouted.

Arthur's guests swarmed about him. They sensed he was about to spontaneously compose a poem—as only he knew how. Without forethought or plan, he simply summoned a completed elegy or stanza that flowed without effort from his mind to whomever stood in his presence. All waited in dead silence.

"A car crashes. It makes a loud noise. It burns up. There is hurt. There is pain. BOOOOMMM! Bad car crash. God speaks. God speaks through the car crash. God says, 'Slow down.' It is too late." Arthur collapsed to the ground.

The guests looked to one another. There was confusion. All were certain that Arthur's spontaneous prose and his collapsing thereafter contained deep

Arthur: An Actuarial Odyssey

meaning. Many felt that it was a sign to build a fire and sacrifice his body to release his tortured soul to a higher plane. It was decided that they must mutilate his shackled bodily form to free his soul from its polluted mortal prison. This woke Arthur. He explained that, in fact, the meaning was far deeper than this and he would need further time to fully discern its true import. His guests untied Arthur from the lamp post, put away the lighter fluid, and took the wads of newspaper from his pants pockets, as the festivities continued on into the night.

The fact was, Arthur was lost. Lost in a world of unfulfilled dreams, broken promises, and an all-consuming, paralyzing void. It had only been a few years earlier that, in an effort to break from his suffocating doldrums, Arthur decided to make a new life for himself. From that time forward, Arthur had dedicated his life to selling life insurance. But it was no good. Arthur could never fully commit himself to his work.

After a while, he discovered that, in fact, the world of life insurance had very little to do with life and much more to do with death. This depressed Arthur. Each day, a new client would sit across his desk and the two would speak in a euphemistic, coded language about some "comprehensive life insurance policy" or "dismemberment clauses." But the whole time the two knew what they were really talking about—how much his client's family could expect to cash in on his rotting corpse.

Arthur: An Actuarial Odyssey

This was not at all what Arthur had imagined when he'd gone into the life insurance business. Arthur's idea of life insurance was just that; insuring the public against suffering an empty, purposeless life. He pictured people coming in and insuring that their children would live happy, gratifying lives. He imagined insurance claims that spawned long, philosophical dialogue in which he and his client could engage in profound introspection, exploring the very essence of our existence and the nature of genuine contentment in a society locked within the confines of a modern, hedonistic world. Instead, too often, he found himself immersed in the grisly details of double homicides and suspicious drownings. This was not for Arthur. After two months he quit the agency to open his own—the Happily Ever After Life Insurance Agency.

Arthur's policy was simple. He would insure anyone up to $100,000 that their life would be a fulfilling and rewarding experience in which they would find deep meaning and purpose. The Happily Ever After Life Insurance Agency would open a policy with no one over ten years old. Furthermore, no one could file a claim before age 55. This was to protect the company from an epidemic of 40-something, mid-life crises. If at age 55, someone had not lived a fulfilling and rewarding life, with deep meaning and purpose, they could then file a Claim of Disenchantment. The claimant would simply need to prove that an impartial third party could reasonably find that she or he had just cause for claiming to be unhappy with their life.

Arthur: An Actuarial Odyssey

After only a week in business, Arthur had over 500 pre-adolescent clients. Parents flocked to Arthur's agency after he'd posted an ad in the local paper imploring them to "help insure their children's future in these troubled and uncertain times." Parents were at first skeptical. But after Arthur showed them a few glossy brochures and shared the details of the policy, most were convinced. Arthur explained that most life insurance agencies focus on death but that his vision was to create an insurance agency that celebrated life. Life insurance was not meant to be some perverse reward for dying, Arthur insisted. Life insurance was meant to protect a person while still living against the scourge of an unfulfilled, meaningless existence.

Soon enough, business was booming. However, Arthur's doubts persisted. He sensed that there may be significant grey area when assessing a person's claim of disenchantment. On the one hand, Arthur craved profound and extended debate and discussion hashing out such matters. On the other hand, his accountant grumbled over the complexity of calibrating actuarial tables to accurately factor in genuine angst, forlornness, and discontent, while weeding out undue resentment, jealousy, and paranoia. His legal counsel, meanwhile, insisted that Arthur exclude claims traced back simply to bad parenting. He told Arthur this would be like offering auto insurance for liability, collision, or whatever.

It became obvious what Arthur had to do. He could not in good faith continue to operate the Happily Ever

Arthur: An Actuarial Odyssey

After Life Insurance Agency without further answers. Both his accountant and his lawyer made this clear. It was crucial that Arthur dedicate himself to discovering the true meaning and purpose of life so as to protect himself from fraudulent claims. Arthur knew they were right. After all, to sell fire insurance one must know about fires. To sell flood insurance one must know about floods. So who was he kidding trying to sell life insurance, when he himself knew so little about life.

Arthur's search for the meaning and purpose of life soon became his mission, his passion, his drive. Along the path to which this led—a path that chose him as much as he chose it—Arthur would weather unspeakable hardships, battle inscrutable foes, and stare down some of humankind's deepest fears and darkest nightmares. Thus it was that Arthur set out to discover the meaning and purpose of life so that he could more adequately prepare to sell insurance for it. His first stop was the bathroom.

Arthur: An Actuarial Odyssey

Chapter Two

Arthur observed quite ingeniously that, though there were a great variety of cultures and peoples around the world, there are still a few basic human needs and proclivities common to all. Understanding these would thus help him to lay bare the most universal and eternal features of human existence. Hence, Arthur knew that the first steps in any search for the meaning and purpose of life must begin with these most basic human needs and proclivities. Indeed, Arthur opened his query with perhaps that most human proclivity of all, the bodily elimination of waste. Arthur was fascinated to learn how entire industries had been built over the last century simply to accommodate the human elimination of waste. There was, as his investigation would uncover, quite a hefty profit to be made from this most natural of human urges.

Indeed, as Arthur looked into matters more deeply he was shocked to learn of a most unpleasant and quite seedy side to the human elimination of waste. The competition for human waste was fierce. Mammoth corporations rose and fell based upon their capacity to

Arthur: An Actuarial Odyssey

facilitate this basic human need. In their craven desire to capture market share, human waste industrialists often engaged in what could be fairly deceptive advertising tactics—tempting the public with their shiny seats and scented rolls of tissue to eliminate their human waste with them. Arthur was disgusted by the whole scene. But he had to know more. He arranged an interview with a leading human waste industrialist, Felix Harper.

The Harper family had been in human waste for over 40 years. Felix's grandfather, the late Claude Harper, had been the first to recognize the potential profit from tapping into the seemingly bottomless reservoir produced by the human elimination of waste. An enormous portrait of Claude Harper adorned the waiting area just outside Felix's office. For all the money he'd earned from people giving him their human waste, Claude had an almost taciturn look about him, with long worry lines creasing his face and heavy bags beneath both eyes. These were no doubt from the many sleepless nights when old Claude lay with his mind fixed on the business of capturing still more of the people's human waste—all for himself!

Arthur developed a fairly unflattering image of Felix Harper as he sat waiting. He pictured an obsessed, corporate monster, installing microphones in the company's bathrooms to better hear each flush—which no doubt fell upon his ears like the ring of a cash register. He imagined Felix's office walls made from baby blue bathroom tiles with a table of free samples—from lemon-scented toilet rolls to cinnamon toast potpourri—

Arthur: An Actuarial Odyssey

cluttering a table along a back wall. Arthur shuddered at the image of walking in to meet Felix. He pictured him extending a cold, hairy hand—still wet from having used one of those 20-second blow dryers—the financial residue of human waste dripping from his every pore, as he spoke excitedly of the fortune he'd gleaned from humans eliminating their waste all for him.

The stale receptionist area was revealing enough, with its literary assortment of *Modern Urinal, Today's Plumber,* and *Toilet World.* The ghoulish portrait of Claude, the patriarch of plungers, confronted all who entered; and just beneath it, the refreshing water cooler inviting, indeed, tempting—nay, beckoning for all to come and take of its bounty. It was, of course, but a coy, mocking hoax—put there in search of fool's gold from those who would drink merely as prelude to eliminate.

Arthur had known that the world created by the human waste industrialists was ugly. Nothing, however, had prepared him for the true depths of its depravity. But Arthur had a mission. And so he steeled himself for his visit with Felix to probe the base reality of human waste elimination perchance to grasp more fully certain intangible truths behind the meaning and purpose of life.

Felix was punctual, one had to grant him that. At precisely 2:15 his office doors swung open and out popped the little man. His diminutive stature at first threw Arthur off. His grandfather's portrait, drawn from the shoulders up, suggested the image of a hulking industrial giant, confidently peering out over his clientele of human

Arthur: An Actuarial Odyssey

waste eliminators. The smaller man before him now seemed to have inherited all of his grandfather's human waste, but none of its luster.

Arthur settled into his patent leather seat across from Felix who looked out from behind his desk with a cheerful smile.

"So how may I help you?" Felix asked.

Arthur explained that he had come to deepen his appreciation for the corporate command over human waste elimination. Felix began to detail the long history of his family's relentless climb in human waste. Arthur listened briefly, then stood and circled his seat before interrupting.

"You just don't get it. Do you?" Arthur shot back.

"Excuse me."

"Don't you see?" Arthur demanded. "This human waste, it's just merchandise to you and your ilk, but for us—those who produce it day in and day out—it's a part of us, a way of life, a basic necessity god damnit!"

"What's the point?" the now uneasy human waste industrialist replied.

"What's the point!?! WHAT'S THE POINT!?! I'll tell you what the point is. You've turned a deeply personal, daily necessity into a profit-driven industry. You've turned a natural and basic, shared, collective, and universal human activity into a private, materialistic ritual, dividing rich and poor human waste eliminators—

Arthur: An Actuarial Odyssey

all out of some carnal corporate greed for our human waste."

"That's outrageous!" the human waste industrialist shrieked.

"Is it now?" Arthur countered. "Well tell me this. All people must eliminate human waste—am I right?"

"Well... sure."

"But all people don't eliminate human waste equally, do they now?"

"I don't know what you're talking about," the now indignant human waste industrialist retorted.

"How can you justify providing some people with the Double Deluxe Model 11 Commode to eliminate *their* waste, while peddling off inferior human waste eliminator devices to other, less wealthy persons?" Arthur demanded.

"That's just the market. Some people have more money to spend than others. So they go for our Double Deluxe Model," responded the human waste industrialist, regaining his confidence.

"I see. So it all comes down to money, eh?" Arthur snidely replied, eyeing his prey.

"What do you mean? *Everything* comes down to money. I mean... what are you—some kind of a Communist?"

Arthur: An Actuarial Odyssey

Arthur shrank back. He remained deeply sensitive to this charge, ever since childhood. He could still hear his mother's scolding words, "What are you some kind of a Communist?" anytime little Arthur neglected his chores. His mother would find him reading in his bed or playing with some friends, instead of washing the car or cleaning his rifle and she would give a long lecture, reminding him that this wasn't the Soviet Union or Red China; how they weren't living on some commune where everyone else was gonna clean up your mess. If little Arthur dared to say anything, he would always get the same response. "Yeah, well why don't you just go back to Russia?"

But Arthur settled his nerves and stuck to the topic. "Everything comes down to money, eh?"

"Sure."

"Even human waste elimination—the most basic and universal human need—has a price."

"In a manner of speaking."

Arthur leaned out over Felix's desk. "WE'RE NOT TALKING TANGERINES HERE! We're talking about the human elimination of waste. It's not like it's a market-driven decision. If ya gotta go, ya gotta go!"

"That's true. But if you wanna use our machines to do it, you have to pay the price."

"I see," an exasperated Arthur replied, slipping back into his seat. "So it doesn't bother you in the slightest that you are using human waste to create a society of the

Arthur: An Actuarial Odyssey

haves and have nots, deciding who will eliminate their human waste where and in how much comfort?"

"The way I see it, by serving my clients' human waste needs—that is to say, their personal sanitation preferences!—I am simply assisting a very natural and market-driven process."

"And so where does it all end?" bemoaned Arthur, leaping to his feet. "This valuing of one person's human waste above another's; this deciding which people will eliminate their human waste where and how; this arbitrary division of society into luxury and economy classes of human waste eliminators?"

"Now see here—," a now infuriated Felix responded. But Arthur interrupted.

"It's all starting to become pretty clear to me now." Arthur sat back down and propped up his feet on the edge of Felix Harper's desk. "Perhaps I should explain."

"Explain what?"

"You see, I'm on a mission. I am seeking the meaning and purpose of life. That is what has brought me to your office today."

"I see," Felix remarked, looking down at his watch. "The meaning and purpose of life."

"Indeed. And I must say that this little talk has been most enlightening."

"How so?"

Arthur: An Actuarial Odyssey

"Let's just say that I never knew the elimination of human waste could be so multi-faceted. To most of us, it's a pretty simple and straightforward affair. But to a rapacious industrialist, such as yourself, human waste is a stepping stone to riches. In your pursuits, our elimination of human waste is a matter of profit and loss, market share, a mere pretext for hawking a host of complementary consumer goods."

"So, who're we hurting?" Felix answered back.

"Maybe no one. Anyway, who knows, heck... maybe we're all to blame. Turning our elimination of human waste needs over to an industry built on corporate greed, forever coveting our precious human waste."

"And how does this explain the meaning and purpose of life?"

"You see, that's the difference between a visionary like myself and a sorry corporate clown like you. Clearly, one cannot find the meaning and purpose of life in the elimination of human waste, per se. However, confronting the ugly corporate reality of human waste elimination does yield certain insights, which, properly reframed, may then point one further along the crooked path to finding the meaning and purpose of life."

"And where might your insights lead you?" Felix wondered.

But before Felix could complete his thought, Arthur bolted from the room in search of his next clue to the

Arthur: An Actuarial Odyssey

meaning and purpose of life. If following the trail of human waste had merely led him to a savage world of greed and avarice, than Arthur knew his quest must move to an even more elementary level. Arthur's quest turned to money—that social scourge, pitting human waste eliminators against one another, rich and poor. If to uncover the meaning and purpose of life one must begin with humanity's most basic needs and proclivities, such as the elimination of human waste, and if to understand the elimination of human waste meant first to understand a multi-billion dollar, profit-soaked industry, than Arthur knew he could not begin with human waste after all.

Indeed, it seemed the generation of human wasted was nothing more than the residue of his *real* object of inquiry—money. Arthur grabbed a taxi and headed across town to meet with his stockbroker, stopping briefly to use a *public* urinal.

Arthur: An Actuarial Odyssey

Chapter Three

Butch was eating lunch with another client and invited Arthur to join them. The client was a hefty Caucasian man in his late 40's. His mid-day nourishment consisted of a steak and cheese sandwich with a side order of fries and a large Pepsi. He and Arthur exchanged niceties with much of the sandwich jammed between his piston-like jaws. Butch's office, modestly adorned, sensibly paneled, and ostentatiously-laden with awards and citations, reflected a life of noteworthy achievement and brazen self-confidence.

It sat on the 14th floor of the Dunmore Building, an office complex dedicated to Philip A. Dunmore—noted philanthropist and humanitarian—who, after a lifetime of pioneering success in the garment industry, had donated his entire life's savings to an orphanage in rural Burma. In keeping with the spirit of giving embodied in Dunmore's selfless act of charity, and following Butch's advice, the Burmese orphan children had used the money to construct the sprawling Dunmore office complex. By means of a fairly straight-forward multiplier effect, as was explained to the young orphans by caring Peace Corps volunteers, the children hoped to have the money

Arthur: An Actuarial Odyssey

trickle back down to them by contributing to a robust world economy and thus benefiting one and all.

Butch and Arthur were old college buddies who life, as it so often does, had sent on separate journeys. Arthur dropped out of college and inherited his father's city-wide chain of male stripper clubs and Butch went on to earn a degree in television/VCR repair from a mail-order trade school, before completing his MBA. Arthur eventually closed the stripper clubs after he was condemned to hell by some local ministers. This followed an incident in which he was badly misquoted in a local newspaper as suggesting that the anti-Christ was merely a victim of bad press.

The issue had first arisen in the question-and-answer period following a luncheon address to the Chamber of Commerce. The full text of Arthur's response clearly reveals him to have said that while he in no way could condone the actions of the anti-Christ, he felt it would be extremely difficult for the anti-Christ to get a fair, public hearing, given such strong anti anti-Christ public sentiment. Arthur had since embarked upon his at times unconventional lifestyle, surviving on the vast wealth generated from those clubs.

He had first met Butch in, of all places, the university cafeteria. Arthur was having the Salisbury steak and sat alone. Butch, still on line and leaning toward the veal, caught site of Arthur from across the crowded lunchroom. He asked if he could join Arthur, who—with an inviting, "it's a free country"—offered Butch a seat. Butch had indeed chosen the veal and Arthur, eyeing his green beans, felt a certain comfort with this new stranger in his life. Butch began, with that awkward, get-to-know-you kind of small talk, asking if Arthur was a new student. Arthur took a contemplatively long swallow of his chocolate milk before confirming Butch's suspicions.

"So what're ya thinkin' of majoring in?" Butch asked.

"Dunno. I'm keepin' my options open, know what I mean?"

"Oh yes, yes," came back a thoroughly confused Butch. "So, where are you from?"

"Here and there."

"I see. And where'd ya grow up?"

Arthur looked up from his tray, gazed past Butch with vacant stare, and asked, "Can any of us ever really say we've 'grown up'?"—capturing that budding metaphysical curiosity that decades later would lead him to Butch's office, seated beside an engorged, middle-aged, Caucasian man in search of the meaning and purpose of life.

"Guess ya got a point," Butch responded. "Well hey, look at the time. Gonna be late. Well... see ya 'round, huh?"

"Right." And with that, though they would not meet again for another two years, a friendship had been forged that would last a lifetime.

Arthur: An Actuarial Odyssey

"So what I can do you for Art?"

Arthur thought carefully before beginning. How to explain his mission? How to condense his mind's query into some easily digestible nugget? How to have Butch enter into his own realm of metaphysical wonder? He decided to begin with his broad project and get Butch's sense of how best to proceed. He explained how he had recently dedicated his life to finding the meaning and purpose of life so that he could more effectively sell insurance for it. He described his earlier efforts and how his searching had sent him on a sojourn into the dark world of human waste elimination.

Finally, he explained, his searching had brought him here to investigate what appeared to be the true object of human waste elimination—profit, the big pay-off. Thus, to continue his search for the meaning and purpose of life down near its very roots he had to find out what this thing called money was all about. Butch had his secretary hold all calls.

"Let me get this straight," Butch mused. "You think money is the basis for the meaning and purpose of life?"

"Not precisely. Let's just say I'm following a trail. When I began I had a sense that human waste elimination was somehow tied to the meaning and purpose of life."

"I see," Butch said, somewhat incredulously.

"Because it's universal Butch. Everybody does it… the world over."

Arthur: An Actuarial Odyssey

"Oh sure, I get it."

"So I figure, find out what's behind this universal human activity, and I'd be halfway home."

"Sure, sure."

"So I found it. It's money. Now I gotta find out what's behind money; what's the next link in the chain?"

"Got it."

"So give it to me straight Butch. I'm ready to take this baby wherever it sails. What's with this money thing?"

"Money. Right. Let's see. You know… you see… the thing is, this thing—money—it's not really such an easy thing to just, you know, talk about straight out like you're suggesting."

"Sounds even more complex than I thought. You'd better begin with the basics."

"Alright, let's see, you wanna know what money is. Well, it's like this. Money is a bunch of pieces of paper that the government prints up so we can buy stuff."

"I see. And where does the government get it?"

"Well, they sort of start out with a set amount and then give it out to the people."

"How do they figure out how much to give people?"

"It depends. You know, how much you make at work. Or how much you get from a dead relative. Or if you win the lottery. Stuff like that."

Arthur: An Actuarial Odyssey

"And then we take the money and we give it to other people to buy stuff," Arthur added.

"That's about it."

"So all these people making money off of human waste do it so they can buy more stuff."

"Somethin' like that."

Arthur was trying to make things make sense in his head. What he had so far was that there was this group of human waste industrialists, who, taking advantage of a basic human proclivity, were helping people to eliminate their waste so that they could get money so that they could buy stuff. Butch assured Arthur that this was a completely rational and socially responsible thing to do.

"But how much stuff do they need precisely?" Arthur continued.

"That's a toughy. Some folks, they settle for a few things. Others, they keep collecting more and more money to buy more and more stuff."

"But in the larger scheme of things they only go after money so they can get a hold of more stuff. They don't really need the money, which is just useless pieces of paper. So what happens when one person collects all the stuff there is to buy?" Arthur wondered.

"Don't talk crazy. It's not possible. There's too much stuff."

Arthur: An Actuarial Odyssey

"Ya gotta open your mind, Butch. Just imagine it. What happens then? There's no more reason to get more money. They've got everything already. Hey, maybe that's it. That's the meaning and purpose of life. To collect as much stuff as you can to break from your need for money!"

"But nobody can *break from the need for money*." Butch insisted.

"Ah hah!" Arthur proclaimed. "It's a vicious circle! The more you collect to free yourself of dependency on money the more dependent you become. That's deep. I like it. I think we're getting somewhere. But there must be a way to break the cycle. The meaning and purpose of life must be tied up in making as much money as you can until you break the cycle."

"What would be the point?" Butch responded. "Let's say you collected all the stuff in the world there is to buy so you don't need any more money. In the end we're all dead anyway. What's all that money gonna buy you then?"

"I think I see where your goin' with this," Arthur rejoined. "I like it. Play up the death angle. You might have something. Death. It's universal just like human waste elimination."

Arthur could kick himself. How could he have missed the connection? It was only natural. The meaning and purpose of life was not to be found in the human elimination of waste, nor in the natural result of the

Arthur: An Actuarial Odyssey

human elimination of waste—money. The meaning and purpose of life could only be found in its contrary form— death. To understand how to succeed in the life insurance industry, Arthur had first to confront and understand its very antithesis—the death industry.

His mission had taken a most provocative turn. And so, Arthur rushed off to question death. As luck would have it, the 153rd Annual National Conference of Morticians was being held at the city's convention center that very weekend. There, within the somber den of dedicated peddlers of bereavement, Arthur hoped to land his next lead.

Arthur: An Actuarial Odyssey

Chapter Four

Arthur paid his 50 dollar entrance fee and headed in. A lecture had just begun in a theater off the main hall, as he arrived. The speaker was reviewing optional methods for collecting past due payments from grieving relatives in a sensitive, yet firm manner; including the delicate subject of digging up delinquent corpses. Arthur took his seat. The main hall was a mammoth space overflowing with dark-suited men, trudging about with fistfuls of brochures and briefcases. Each was pinned to a light green name tag announcing oneself to the others. Most of the name tags identified the towns in which a mortician bought dead bodies. Arthur wasn't certain how to fill his out. He settled on "Arthur–Freelancer."

Half listening to the speaker's impassioned discussion of the proper storing of a re-possessed corpse in an undisclosed location until final payment, Arthur sat

Arthur: An Actuarial Odyssey

leafing through a few brochures he'd taken from a back table:

The first had a plain cover, with a simple message: "Are You Properly Planning Your Own Death?"

Another asked: "Death: What Are the Options?"

An olive green brochure read simply: "So, You Want to Cremate Your Family"

Lastly, for the environmentalists, there was a small brochure announcing a bold vision:

"The Socially Responsible Mortician: Building a Better World One Casket at a Time"

As best Arthur could make out, there was one common theme emerging: how to cash in on death. There seemed an eerie resemblance, at some level, between the human death industry and the human waste industry.

Thumbing through the conference program, Arthur found two or three lecture topics of particular interest. He circled one later that afternoon on "Population Control and the Mortician's Right to a Free Market: Colliding Interests?" before stepping into an adjoining conference room to grab some java and mingle. Arthur maneuvered his way to a corner of the room where he was exchanging business cards with Edward Edwardson III. Fumbling with his jacket pocket, a pack of Marlboro's fell out onto the floor, whereupon six or seven morticians leapt past one another to hand Arthur their card. A grateful Arthur turned back to Edward Edwardson.

Arthur: An Actuarial Odyssey

Edward, by all appearances, was fairly typical of those attending the conference. His eyes revealed a caring, sensitive soul—able to provide comfort; to feel another's pain; to help a mourning loved one find peace and solace. Arthur asked how long he'd been buying dead bodies and he could sense Edward's mood take a turn. Edward, it seemed, was about to open up to Arthur. Edward explained that the popular characterization of morticians as "buyers of dead bodies" was not precisely accurate. Confused and hoping to re-focus the conversation, a flustered Arthur made a desperate attempt at mortuary humor. He noted that if "old Eddie" wasn't just burying *dead* ones, not to worry, his lips were sealed. Edward suddenly spotted an old friend across the room and politely excused himself. Arthur re-gathered himself and sought out further representatives of the death industry.

Before he could narrow in on anyone, a fellow mingler spotted Arthur and approached. His name was Rick Astro. Rick was not a mortician. Rick was a male model hired to help display a new line of environmentally responsible caskets. This explained why he seemed so over-dressed. Arthur explained that he too was a mere civilian here among the gaggle of morticians and that he had come in his efforts to discover the meaning and purpose of life. The two sat for a while by the cheese dip, watching others pass by and exchanging thoughts on the meaning and purpose of life. Rick's brief but eventful stint as a commercial corpse had given him some

Arthur: An Actuarial Odyssey

important insights with respect to life and death. Arthur listened intently.

For Rick, attitude was everything. To truly be dead was a matter of proper motivation. As a case in point, Rick felt that the Zeus Flyer Casket that he had been modeling earlier in the day, with its soft velvet interior and spongy cushioning provided just the right level of comfort for getting into character. Rick felt that being dead in-and-of-itself was not enough. One needed the right conditions to fully appreciate and resolve one's self to the state of being dead. As he spoke, a small man in a silver-blue suit rushed past waving a clip board. He called out to Rick, letting him know he had five minutes until he was due back in the showroom.

To Rick, the death industry served a vital service of demonstrating to people that being dead meant more than simply not having a pulse. Certain basic accouterments came with—in fact defined—being dead. Without proper accessorizing, one truly was *just a corpse*. Done right, however, Rick was convinced that a simple corpse could become a fully dead human being. It was this basic insight, Rick surmised, that if applied to life more generally could lead Arthur to many of his answers. The meaning and purpose of life wasn't just having a pulse. The meaning and purpose of life was having a pulse and knowing what to do with it. But Rick was out of time. For Rick Astro it was time to die.

Arthur came away from his meeting with Rick impressed. Now running late, he needed to rush to make

Arthur: An Actuarial Odyssey

the afternoon lecture. On the way, however, he could not pass up stopping by the showroom. There, fourth casket from the left, Rick's body lay in state. Passers-by noted the caskets' durable design, its intricate detail, its shiny finish. Arthur saw only a brilliant performance.

The speaker was beginning her lecture as Arthur hustled in. Arthur noted the speaker's extensive preparation and sensed that hers would be a sterling presentation on obstacles to a free market in dead bodies. The speaker presented numerous charts and graphs. Her first slide broke down the yearly government budgets for family planning over the last three decades. Next she detailed the number of dead bodies purchased in the country over the same period beside the *potential* number of dead bodies had the government not pursued its anti-mortician policies.

A soft murmur moved through the crowd. The speaker informed the room of stunned morticians that huge lobbying efforts were behind this drastic fall in market share. Powerful forces were organized and poised to cut back even further on the country's supply of dead bodies.

The crowd grew surly and there were calls for retribution. The speaker tried to temper the mortician's rising fury. She explained that those forces aligned against them were quite varied. Some groups stood out more than others, such as the consumer advocacy fanatics urging governments to force automakers to build safer cars and even forcing people—through big government regulation—to wear seat belts, costing morticians

Arthur: An Actuarial Odyssey

countless customers. A mortician toward the front threw a chair up onto the stage yelling hysterically. The speaker was able to settle things down and moved to another chart. This tracked the number of persons whose dead bodies could not be purchased due to government policies improving auto safety.

But it did not end there, the speaker added. If it wasn't consumer advocacy fanatics it was the militant—largely lesbian-organized—anti-family, anti-dead-body-free-market, so-called pro-choice activists. This movement alone was responsible for one of the largest drops in the number of marketable dead bodies to date. The speaker was careful to point out two important aspects to consider. It was not simply this "fringe" group's efforts to legalize abortion, though this was certainly quite damaging to the market in dead bodies since it simply snuffed out the development of a potential dead body before it even had a chance to fully form.

However, there was a yet more insidious, less publicized aspect of this powerful lobby's campaign. This was its efforts to enhance pre-natal care. Their largely successful efforts to harness resources and focus government policy on the survival of malnourished, underweight infants had eliminated a vital market which had traditionally helped counter down periods of the year. The crowd seethed. A row of morticians in the rear demanded names and addresses.

The speaker was able to bring the riot-bent mob of morticians back down to an orderly rumble with her

Arthur: An Actuarial Odyssey

announcement that there were, in fact, several noteworthy, positive trends. They could still count on a good number of advocacy groups who championed a mortician's right to an unfettered market in dead bodies. The tobacco lobby, rebounding from hard times, was beginning to get back on its feet. This remained a sensitive matter. A palpable, lingering hostility continued among segments of the mortician community over the tobacco industry's recent push into third world markets.

Efforts to expand the tobacco market by addicting third world adolescents troubled many morticians who knew that they could not match the foreign competition. It was true that the industry had made considerable inroads addicting younger and younger smokers in their home market, providing morticians with a predictable market boom. However, many still felt that if the tobacco was grown here, subsidized here, and manufactured here, than it was only right that the profit from the resulting dead bodies should remain here as well.

Additionally, the strongest advocates of a free market in dead bodies, working through their exhaustive campaigns for the protection of yet-formed dead bodies, the self-styled pro-life movement, was still going strong. For example, the speaker assured the uneasy crowd that the pro-life movement had made a careful study of the earlier civil rights movement and was masterfully employing the tactics and strategies of that era. Pro-life leaders had learned to isolate specific targets and maximize their impact.

Arthur: An Actuarial Odyssey

Thus, just as earlier good citizens had forcefully stood in school house doorways to block certain undesirables from entering, today right-to-lifers block entry to medical offices where the development of budding dead bodies is terminated. Just as earlier a network of terror—formed by simple, common folk—was required to thwart the efforts of the undesirables to vote and what not, the pro-life movement had embarked upon a sophisticated network of terror and intimidation, employing the tried and true tactics of the earlier era—including fire bombings, physical assaults, and assassination.

Increased opportunities for tobacco addiction along with advances in the movement to force women to give birth to fully-formed, prospective dead humans were important victories that morticians everywhere should take heart in, the speaker announced with glee as she came to her rousing close. In conclusion, the speaker sought to re-assure the crowd, reminding them that death—as Providence had so generously granted—was a constant. One must not despair at momentary market losses. What was important was to continuously help shape the dead body market of tomorrow by expanding lobbying efforts to combat those pushing to put limits on the market in dead bodies today.

The crowd rose to its feet in thunderous applause. The speaker strode from the podium reminding one and all of their duty to remain ever-vigilant in their resolve as morticians to maintain a free and open market in dead bodies, steeped in the proud principles for which we'd fought a revolution and two world wars. Arthur felt deeply moved.

In his emotional state he decided to unwind a bit at the cocktail bar. With a heavy sigh he leaned out over his gin and tonic, stirring it lifelessly. A dark-suited, quiet man ordered a whiskey sour, taking the stool beside him. The two exchanged glances. By his badge Arthur knew his name was Todd. Arthur took a hard swallow, sat straight up and turned to the quiet man. He asked if he was here for the conference. He was. He asked if he'd been a practicing mortician long. He had. He asked if he found the conference enjoyable. He did. He asked if his plans were to attend all three days. They were. The quiet man drank his whiskey sour. Arthur drank his gin.

The quiet man turned to Arthur.

"I know why you're here."

"Excuse me?" a nervous but intrigued Arthur responded.

"I can see it in your eyes," the quiet man said stirring his drink and staring indifferently past Arthur's right shoulder.

"Is that so?" Arthur answered, fingering the end of his tie. "Tell me then, what is it you see?"

"I've been to enough of these conferences to know just who and what you are."

"Really?" Arthur looked the quiet man up and down, took another swallow and leaned back coolly in his stool.

Arthur: An Actuarial Odyssey

The quiet man continued. "Your kind is a common sight at these conferences. You want information."

Arthur eyed the quiet man. "I suppose you could say that."

"You won't find it here." The quiet man continued to stare past Arthur.

"And what makes you so confident?"

"You're lookin' for the meaning and purpose of life?"

"Well... yeah. I mean, you might say that."

"There's always one or two each year. You think because we're morticians, because we deal with the ultimate ending every day, we have some kind of a clue about things."

"So what're ya tellin' me? Wrong crowd? You don't know?"

"I'm not sayin' that. Of course, we know."

Arthur leaned in, lowering his voice. "You know the meaning of life?"

"No."

"Then what are you saying?" Arthur asked.

"I know who knows."

Arthur took out a pen and notepad to take down names. But the quiet man motioned him to put them away.

Arthur: An Actuarial Odyssey

"He's long since dead," the quiet man confided.

"I see."

"He was a fire fighter. I laid him to rest ten years back, this very week. He was 35, a family man. He'd been a fire fighter nearly 15 years. One day, the station got a call. A house caught fire on Houston Street. A small boy was trapped on the third floor; not two years old. By the time they arrived the flames were too hot for the ladder to reach the third story window. The fire crew stood below helpless; horrified by the terror-stricken cries of the child burning alive in the inferno. His half-mad mother wailed and kicked and screamed, desperately wanting to rush back into the crumbling building. Jim knew his chances were slim. But the terrible, tortured cries were too much to bear. He pictured his own two-year old crying out his final frantic calls for help and he knew what he had to do. Jim grabbed an ax and dashed blindly into the burning structure. The fire fighters trained their hoses on the frightful flames. And when the fires' embers at last died out… when the final charred remains smoldered into ash… there was heard a little boy's cry from within the blackened ruins. No one knows just how he reached the child. And no one ever will. Because there, only feet from the frightened child protected only by a fire suit and oxygen mask that saved his life, lay the burned remains of a fire fighter named Jim."

Arthur fell back off his bar stool. "My God."

Arthur: An Actuarial Odyssey

"You see, my friend, only a man like that, a man who would face those flames to save another's life could tell you about the meaning and purpose of life."

Arthur stared in silence.

"Pity that men like that lack the luxury of time to delve into deep philosophical conversation about the motive or meaning behind their selfless, life-saving act."

Arthur slumped forward, emotionally comatose.

"Fortunately, however, in the case of Jim, he did leave behind a final note."

"You mean he managed to scribble his final thoughts, while facing death, on some miraculously surviving scrap of paper tucked within the child's protective fire suit."

"Don't be insane. It turned out Jim was a pathological gambler who'd lost his family's entire savings a few days earlier. Depressed and suicidal, he wrote out a note declaring that he was no good to anyone. He'd failed his wife, his family, and himself. He wanted only to end it all. So the real tragedy of the whole episode, once the insurance company found the note, was that Jim's heroic rescue mission was turned into as a classic suicide-by-firefighting; so his wife and kids were out the family savings he had lost along with any life insurance claims. The fire fighters association took back all his awards and citations for bravery and now use his story as a lesson for young recruits to avoid work when feeling depressed or dealing with personal troubles."

Arthur: An Actuarial Odyssey

"Oh my God, that's horrible. Where's the justice? Where's the sense of it all?"

"You see that's how I reacted. But then something got me thinking."

"What was that?" a sullen Arthur asked, ordering another gin and tonic.

"I was standing in the rear of the room during Jim's funeral service counting heads and noticing that there were six more attendees than had been planned for, forcing us immediately to change to a buffet-style lunch, when I noticed the minister, seated behind the person giving the eulogy, starting to nod off. And that's when it struck me."

"What? What struck you?" Arthur asked, as he motioned the bartender to refresh the quiet man's drink.

"Don't you see, the man's life had been such a total and complete failure that even God was bored. I've seen it before. It's not something morticians really talk about in mixed company, but ministers falling asleep is actually quite common. Like God is channeling a message."

"A message eh. What kind'a message?"

"I'm bored."

"God is bored?"

"Precisely. Seen it too many times."

"Really."

Arthur: An Actuarial Odyssey

"All I'm trying to say is I think you're talkin' to the wrong people. The way I see it, if death is just a big bore to God, the answers must be somewhere else."

"I catch you're meaning. But where? Where else can I turn?"

Just then, a voice called out from the shadows.

"Excuse my indiscretion." A tall stranger made stepped out from behind a row of plastic ferns and approached the two. "I couldn't help overhearing your concerns."

"And?" Arthur shot back defensively.

"And... I think I might be of some assistance."

The tall stranger had a wayward look about him. His stride was long and confident. His voice was deep and full. His hair was black and combed. If this tall stranger had something to offer, Arthur wanted to hear it. The quiet stranger hurriedly paid his tab and excused himself. Others seated near the bar retreated to more distant tables. A man at the jukebox stood studying the selections when suddenly the tall stranger halted in his tracks, raised his right arm and, without turning his head, called out for the man to play "11c"—twice. The soulful sounds of Michael Bolten's slightly strained rendition of the Whitney Houston smash hit "I'm Every Woman" filled the bar, as the tall stranger took the stool beside Arthur's.

"Have we met?" Arthur asked.

"That's not important."

Arthur: An Actuarial Odyssey

"You say you have some information?" Arthur continued.

"I do."

The tall stranger reached down, striking a match on his left boot, lighting a cigarette, and offering one to Arthur. Arthur declined. The tall stranger lay his elbows on the bar and took a long, contemplative drag before turning back to Arthur.

"You say you wanna know the meaning of life?"

"That's right?"

"And you think you can handle it?" the stranger teased.

"Just don't waste my time," Arthur snapped, downing the last of his gin and tonic. The tall stranger looked Arthur over.

"Alright. I'll keep it simple," the tall stranger answered. A long and dramatic pause followed. The tall stranger leaned back from the bar, turned squarely to face Arthur and stared with a burning intensity into his eyes. "Find God," he offered. The tall stranger took a final puff, tossed his cigarette, and ambled for the door. The sea of morticians parted to let him pass.

"There's just one problem!" Arthur called out.

"Oh?" the tall stranger answered, pausing in the doorway without turning back.

Arthur: An Actuarial Odyssey

"I have deeply conflicted religious views. In general, I see God as the imagined, material manifestation of an alienated society suffering from mass psychosis in desperate search for unfulfilled truth and meaning in their lives."

The tall stranger stood frozen in his tracks. A hush fell over the bar. Raising an eyebrow, he turned slowly in his tracks, his gaze now fixed on Arthur. With slow, deliberate steps he made his way back over to Arthur's stool. All was silent but for his steel-toed boots brushing across the bar room's polished floor. He stood over Arthur.

"You sayin' you're a Godless atheist."

"Well, your phrasing seems somewhat redundant. But yes, that captures the general flavor."

"Well let me ask you something."

Arthur sat with a smug, wry smile.

"Do you believe in the existence of automobiles?"

"Certainly."

"And you believe in automobiles because somebody sells them to people who then drive them, right?"

"Something like that."

"And so, one could say, because there are automobile salespeople there are automobiles."

"I suppose."

Arthur: An Actuarial Odyssey

"Well, it's no different with God."

"How so?"

"There are ministers, people who sell God, as it were. Therefore, there is a God."

"I must say I've never heard anyone put it quite that way before. I suppose, you may have something of a point."

"Certainly," the tall stranger answered. And with that, the tall stranger disappeared back into the shadows as the bar crowd reoccupied their seats.

Arthur was beside himself. Here at last was definitive proof for the existence of God. There could be only one thing to do. He had to immediately seek out the most commercially successful salesperson for God to dig up further answers. At that very hour the Reverend Isaac Spindlestick was completing the taping of his latest infomercial for God. Reverend Spindlestick was easily among God's wealthiest salespersons. He had been marketing God and His products for nearly 22 years and could now be seen nightly in five out of the top six media markets across the country. Arthur knew he had to find this paragon of Righteous marketing and get some answers. The Reverend's press secretary said he could squeeze Arthur in the next day around 2:30 that afternoon, but it would have to be quick.

"It's a date," Arthur confirmed and turned on his heal.

Arthur: An Actuarial Odyssey

Chapter Five

That night Arthur prepared tirelessly for his brief encounter with God's top-grossing marketer. The press secretary sent him a comprehensive press packet and he perused the Reverend's elegant, yet tasteful, catalogue of Gospel-Inspired Kitchenware. But Arthur felt he had enough background. He just wanted a chance to sit down with the Reverend and cut to the chase.

The two met the next afternoon. Each stretched their hand to the other and the preliminaries were over. Arthur explained that he'd come for information. He detailed his mission and why he had chosen Reverend Spindlestick in particular, God's wealthiest peddler, to advance his search. The Reverend appeared impressed. He leaned forward smiling and pulled a handgun from his top drawer. The Reverend's assistant, who'd been standing by the rear door, now backed out of the room. Arthur fumbled a bit with his notes and continued with rapt attention.

"So ya wanna know the meaning and purpose of life, is it?"

The Reverend shoved a cartridge round into the pistol's hand grip and laid it on the table.

Arthur nodded.

"Simple," the Reverend answered. "Shoot me."

"Sir?"

"Take the gun. Point it at me. And shoot."

"I'm not sure I completely follow."

"I'm not saying to hit me. Just shoot over my head."

"I'm not sure just exactly what we'll be accomplishing with that maneuver, sir."

"Let's just see. Shall we?"

The Reverend handed the weapon to a perspiring and reticent Arthur. Then, aiming just past the Reverend's right temple, Arthur emptied the magazine and put the still smoking pistol back on the desk.

"Something like that?" Arthur asked.

The Reverend nodded, quite shaken. Composing himself, the Reverend continued, "Now... how do you feel?"

"Confused."

"Confused about what?"

Arthur: An Actuarial Odyssey

"Well, I'm not really sure why you had me do that," replied Arthur.

"If you were confused why did you do it?" asked the Reverend.

"Gosh, I don't know. You seemed to know what you were doing."

"Of course I did."

"And what were you doing?" continued Arthur.

"Asking you to try and shoot my head off."

"But why, what possessed you to ask me that?" asked Arthur.

"It's a little test I do with wayward souls who happen across my path. Now, admittedly you are the first to actually go through with pulling the trigger, let alone emptying the weapon—but we'll worry about the clean-up later. No one before even took the gun from me."

"And what have we learned?" Arthur wondered. "How did this experience advance our understanding?"

Members of the Reverend's staff cautiously filed back in to inspect the scene.

"Indeed," the Reverend pondered. "This has me wondering the same thing. Let's reconstruct the situation. You enter, ask the meaning of life, try to shoot my head off, and I survive."

Arthur: An Actuarial Odyssey

"You sort of skipped over the part where you *told* me to shoot at you in that scenario."

"Well... at any rate, I think the matter is clear."

His staff now quietly circled behind Arthur from the rear of the room.

"How's that?"

"God has chosen to speak to me through you. That, no doubt, is why He sent you here this afternoon."

"And what has God told you? What is His message? Does it cover the meaning and purpose of life?"

"Indeed, indeed... the message."

The Reverend stalled, as his men crept into position to snare Arthur from behind.

"Well perhaps it was best recorded in the Book of Ezekiel, chapter eight, verse one," the Reverend continued, "where it is written: 'In the sixth year, in the sixth month, on the fifth of the month, as I was sitting in my house with the elders of Judah sitting in front of me, the hand of the sovereign Lord seized me. As I watched, I noticed a form that appeared—'"

In a flash the Reverend's men swooped in. Though Arthur heard no trumpets and saw no angels, he was about to feel the hand of God reach out to him. This, however, he would only piece together much later. For now, he felt himself lifted up by a burly, 300-pound church usher who grabbed him by the scruff of the neck

Arthur: An Actuarial Odyssey

and foisted him through the blessed church gates and out into the gutter.

For Arthur, this was rock bottom. Where next to turn he did not know.

Arthur: An Actuarial Odyssey

Chapter Six

Alas, Arthur felt no closer to his riddle's solution than at his journey's start. He had probed the secrets behind some of humankind's most revered social institutions; the human waste industry, the money industry, the death industry, and now God's industry. All had left him woefully unfit to grasp the ultimate meaning and purpose of life. He was beginning to wonder if he would *ever* find the answers he needed in order to sell life insurance. Dejected and alone, Arthur roamed the city streets, bumming cigarettes and stopping to down the occasional bourbon or straight whiskey.

Several hours later, drunk and disoriented, he stumbled upon a bar loud with laughter and profanity. He pushed his way in and cut a path through the rollicking Sodom and Gomorrah to an empty barstool. The crowd was strangely agitated, and Arthur fought to catch the attention of the bartender. He couldn't make sense of the oddly excited commotion, at first. Looking about, he was

Arthur: An Actuarial Odyssey

startled to spy a pair of burly bar flies to his left drinking a warm, oily-looking, green substance from a couple of beer mugs.

Looking across the bar further, it became clear that *everyone* in the so-called "bar" was boisterously downing a mugful of this same thick, green substance. The bartender's loud bark of "How many!" over the boisterous crowds rolling laughter hit Arthur by surprise.

"One!" he shot back.

Before he could re-think his options, a warm mug slid down the bar, landing in front of him. Arthur gestured to ask, "How much?"—rather than screaming above the gregarious mob.

The bartender shouted, "500!"

Arthur, unamused, shouted back, "500 *what?*"

The bartender, who had carried on this half verbal/half pantomime drama from a distance, now moved closer.

"Bucks, funny man. 500 bucks."

Arthur pushed back from his "drink" and crawled down from the stool. Evidently, his earlier drinking had caught up with him in a most peculiar and unaccustomed fashion.

He grabbed the back a chair to hold himself steady and began to leave. Five-hundred dollar green slime drinks and an obnoxiously hyper crowd were enough to call it a night. Though it was not so much the *actual* loudness of

Arthur: An Actuarial Odyssey

the crowd, as the *collective* loudness of the crowd that riled him. It was as if they were all sharing the same joke in unison, laughing on cue—gasping, pausing, passing comments—all in synch, though everyone was dispersed quite randomly throughout the bar; seated or standing in separate small groups or off alone. Then, at last, Arthur caught on to the peculiar object of the surreal bar crowd's fascination. The raucous, pulsating, rock music pounding off the walls and floor had initially distracted him. What he had assumed to be monitors for music videos set out in different corners of the bar were, in fact, displaying videos—but videos unlike any he had ever seen.

Everyone among the green-slime drinking, bar crowd studied the monitors intently in the midst of their frenzied fun. From a distance the image was hazy, but moving closer, Arthur was dismayed to discover that the monitors projected the graphic details and intricacies of cell division within simple organisms. Arthur postponed his exit. Passing on an offer to "just try a sip" from an especially exuberant partyer's brew, he sat to examine what so fascinated this unruly bunch.

Each time a cell successfully divided the entire bar would howl with laughter and many would offer a toast, slapping each other on the back. Then, when the narrator introduced new video footage of yet another cell preparing to divide, the crowd would fall deathly quiet. Inebriated celebration and madcap shenanigans were replaced by furrowed brows and tense, darting glances. Couples would nervously embrace, the faint-of-heart

Arthur: An Actuarial Odyssey

would draw closer to their mug—until, by the miracle of nature, the cell successfully divided and again the crowd would explode with joyous pandemonium. Arthur sat through three or four of these "miracles" before turning for some explanation of this ritual from a bubbly young man in a navy green, woolen, Serape poncho with matching shoes.

Still framing the question in his mind, Arthur was interrupted by a teary-eyed patron caught up in a particularly touch-and-go division who leaned over—without taking his eyes off the screen—and asked for napkins. Handing them off, Arthur caught the last few words on the napkins logo—"…Cycle Bar and Grill." He snatched another. Along the bottom in bright, green letters was printed the bar's full name—"The Extended Life-Cycle Bar and Grill." Arthur had stumbled into a life-extension bar. No wonder the drinks were so expensive, he thought.

The irony of it all, Arthur thought to himself. After failing so miserably in his search for the meaning and purpose of life, he had somehow landed in a bar overflowing with those obsessed with prolonging their lives. Here they had come to gather and to find solace in the shared spectacle of simple cell division. Arthur knew he still had much to learn. For this, he would need more time. So, copying the time and place for the next gathering of the local chapter of the Healthier-than-Thou Life-Extenders, he made plans not to miss it.

Arthur: An Actuarial Odyssey

The life-extenders met in a crowded studio apartment on the West side of town. Arthur was running late and nearly dropped the button he was handed as he hurried in, before taking a seat in the kitchen doorway. The button, reading: "Want to Join the Detour of Life? Ask Me How," was at first upside-down, until a fellow Healthier-than-Thou life-extender helped out. The meeting got off to a confused start as several relatives of a death row inmate, who had apparently been misinformed about the nature of the group, politely excused themselves.

Arthur studied the faces all about him. They seemed young, vibrant, eager to live life to its fullest. Indeed, the crowd was a genuine cross section of society. Why, there was Phil the baker, Bob the banker, Mary the policewoman, and Arnold the circus performer. All had answered a calling difficult to put into words. For each, to probe her or his own psyche would reveal not one but one hundred reasons for such urgings. But a true life-extender did not question their calling. A true life-extender simply followed their passions, threw caution to the wind, and lived a life of infinite wonder and adventure.

Arthur sat back and the meeting was called to order. There was, alas, first some bad news. A fellow life-extender from an out-of-town chapter had apparently gone off his rigid Healthier-than-Thou Life-Extension regiment and was promptly struck by a bus. A mournful hush fell over the room, in memory of their fallen colleague. The speaker exhorted one and all that this once more stood as testament to the grave consequences for

Arthur: An Actuarial Odyssey

those who wavered. Life-extension was a 24-hour a day calling, he explained. All listened intently, still grieving their collective loss.

The speaker was a small, energetic man who could light up the room with his out-going, in-your-face-Mr.-Death attitude. Arthur was entranced. Today's discussion was to address the widespread abuse by members of their gums, entitled, "Dental Floss: Where the Myths End and the Truth Begins." One could see the theme truly struck a chord. Pens and notepads were whipped out. The speaker sat on the edge of the arm of a sofa with a contemplative look—steeling herself for her role as messenger. All looked on. She rested her chin on the back of her knuckles, let out a long, life-extending sigh and began.

"Fellow Healthier-than-Thou life extenders, the message for today is not an easy one. Oh no, if only it were. If only there were a simple way—a short-cut solution—to get people to think more seriously about their gums."

Arthur could feel his gums decaying as she spoke.

"If only there were an easy way to let you all know that—A LIFE WITH ROTTED GUMS IS NOT A LIFE WORTH EXTENDING!!!"

The speaker had chosen to shout these final thoughts at the top of her lungs. A very effective technique thought Arthur, as he tried to pry the apartment's cat from his lap.

Arthur: An Actuarial Odyssey

"So you all think you know how to floss? Well, let me tell you something! Flossing isn't just some mundane part of a daily routine. Flossing is a WAY OF LIFE!!!"

How true this had always been in his own experience, Arthur thought.

"You there! Yeah, you, with that serious, I'm-gonna-live-forever look."

Immediately everyone stood.

"No, no, this one, with the goofy sweater." She was referring to an older man seated in the front with a goofy sweater.

"How old are you?"

The man said he was 77. Everyone stood and applauded his remarkably well-preserved form.

"Let me compliment you on your remarkably well-preserved form. Tell me how often do you floss?"

He said that he flossed twice a day; three times if he not competing in a triathlon that week.

"I see. And do you in fact still have all of your original teeth?"

He did.

"My point exactly!"

Everyone applauded wildly, as a clueless Arthur whistled and cheered.

"So you see fellow life-extenders—"

Arthur: An Actuarial Odyssey

Suddenly, from the far corner a horrific shriek went out.

"Informer! Informer!"

A radio inside the jacket of the man beside Arthur went off: "We've got wheat germ at six o'clock. Third row. Proceed with caution. Repeat, proceed with caution."

This, unfortunately, was an all-too-common occurrence within life-extension circles, as Arthur would later come to learn. Zealously guarded secrets of the trade were constantly being pilfered by organizational spies reporting back to their respective life-extension clans. Wheat germ, as all Healthier-than-Thou clan members knew, had been banished from member diets after the devastating internal Bailwax Report in 1987. Only a spy unfamiliar with the latest clan dietary strictures could have brought such an abomination into the midst of pure Healthier-than-Thou life-extenders.

The spy's punishment was cruel beyond words. Held down by four Healthier-than-Thou life-extenders, he was forced to reveal his clan affiliation upon penalty of being force-fed the wheat germ. When he wouldn't talk, the brutal punishment was administered—one spoonful at a time. Arthur couldn't bear the sight. An audible gasp went through the Healthier-than-Thou life-extenders who were all too familiar with the Bailwax Report and its irrefutable findings with respect to wheat germ and its complete lack of life-extending nutrients.

Arthur: An Actuarial Odyssey

Order was being restored, members returning to their seats, and the intruder had been removed when, from across the room, near the tropical fishbowl, like a vision, he saw her—she with the long, flowing, jet-black hair, those deep-set hazel brown eyes, the two huge, protruding—almost elephant-like—ears, offset by a dazzling whiter than white smile. Arthur felt emotions he had never emoted. He felt desire he had never desired. He felt needs he had never needed. For Arthur it was clear. This was lust at first sight. Not a depraved, carnal lust, but a healthy, natural, lifetime-of-orgasms-together kind of lust. He had to meet this beauty, this goddess, this green slime-drinking woman of his dreams.

In the confusion of people returning to their seats, Arthur slyly made his way over. Much like a melodramatic 1940s Hollywood musical, as he sashayed across the room, her eyes met his—and for a second that felt like hours—they shared a moment. Unlike a melodramatic 1940s Hollywood musical, in mid-sashay, Arthur tripped over a ritualistic empty urn—which each life-extender carried with them to signify their not being dead—and sailed headlong into the fish tank, landing beside a flapping blow fish by the feet of this vision of beauty. Years from then they would look back on this moment and laugh, laugh, laugh. At the time, however, she could only scream, scream, scream, as fellow life-extenders worked to pull shards of glass from her profusely bleeding lower leg.

Arthur: An Actuarial Odyssey

Rushing her to the hospital, having lost nearly half a pint of blood, Arthur knew she too had felt the magic. When leaving to join her at the hospital he turned to another life-extender and asked, "But what is her name? By what shall I call her?"

"Puma!" a voice called back. "Puma Wawa!"

Puma Wawa, its mere mention sent fiery sparks throughout his body. There was a bond between them that no power on Earth could sever. Seeing her there, strapped to an artificial respirator, an IV racing fluids to her weakened frame, Arthur felt a tinge of embarrassment—sensing that she was shamelessly undressing him with her eyes, as she faded in and out of consciousness. Never having spoken a word, never having shared a thought, the two now each possessed a burning passion and unquenchable desire to be in one another's arms, to rip the constricting clothes from each other's bodies, to feel their hot, pounding morning breath burning one another's nostrils, as they woke from an endless night of unbridled sexual energy. For now, however, their passions must be held in abeyance. The doctors had only recently upgraded Puma's condition and moved her from the ICU.

She remained in the hospital another week. Arthur would arrive early each morning to bring his love a bright, red rose. He would soothe her afternoons with a new poem that he had spent the night's late hours composing, beside a single burning candle, which he said was like their love—a flaming passion which even after it melted could be re-shaped and lit again. Though the

Arthur: An Actuarial Odyssey

doctors had her on a strict liquid diet, he would sneak in little health treats he'd made from the *Healthier-than-Thou Life-Extenders Cookbook*. And through it all the two would talk, and laugh, and giggle, and cry, and then talk some more repeating the entire cycle.

By the end of Puma's hospital stay, the two felt as if they'd known one another their entire lives. Where had he been all her life, she asked. Prompting Arthur to ask what did she mean where had *he* been all *her* life, where the hell had *she* been, which led, at last, to their first fight. Like all young lover's caught up in the innocence of new-found passion, the two made up by refusing to speak to one another for several months.

At last, their time apart grew too great for Arthur to bear, and he made the first move to rekindle their burning romance. His opportunity came at the local delicatessen where he next saw Puma again. She had number 99. He had 98. The two stood stony-eyed, each waiting their turn for the deli-man. As number 98 was called out, Arthur could hold back his passions no more. Puma had penciled in the number "8" and was now brazenly pushing past Arthur with a forged ticket. Arthur went berserk. Waiving a wiener in one hand and a bag of chips in the other, he ripped into Puma.

"You cheat! How could you!?! I was here first! I'm number 98!"

"Whatta ya talkin' about hot-dog man, says 98 right here. Read it and weep!"

Arthur: An Actuarial Odyssey

"It's a fake!" A hushed silence fell over the crowd pressed up against the deli counter. These were serious accusations.

"Are you insane? What do I look like some kind of common line-jumping freak!?!"

"All I'm saying is I've got number 98 right here, so you can't have it there."

"I can't believe this. You must be some kind of psychopathic loon."

"Why I oughta make you eat those words. I oughta—"

But before he could finish his sentence the two were locked in each other's mad embrace, lips passionately pressed together between tearful apologies. How could they have been so blind, both wondered. For each, life without the other was unthinkable. Puma and Arthur left the deli to begin a new life.

The pair dated for nearly three months before deciding they needed more time together and so took an apartment. Puma was an unemployed third grade teacher, who'd been an active life-extender for almost 11 years. She said she hadn't held a teaching job for nearly two years and was re-thinking her career goals, given her recently discovered loathing for people who ask too many questions. As Puma explained it, with third-graders basically all day there were nothing but questions. And always such stupid questions. Not like they couldn't figure out by themselves what the hell time it was or how

Arthur: An Actuarial Odyssey

to tie a goddamn shoe. And by the time she'd answered all the most basic curiosities, they'd just ship the kids out and bring in a new batch of clueless midgets.

She'd been fired from her last teaching job when they said she'd crossed the line. After the fifth student in the first week asked her what time it was she stormed into a class of second-graders, screaming hysterically at the teacher and asking if she knew "how the hell to tell time," or was able "to tie her own damn shoes." And, if she could, why didn't she bothered to explain any of this to her dumb-as-paste students. They said she needed time to rest. But every third-grade teacher knew what "time to rest" meant. Maybe she just didn't have what it took to handle third-graders. Arthur listened and tried to understand.

He told her of his own occasional feelings of inadequacy. His inability to order food when staring into a clown's face at the local drive-through restaurant without giggling uncontrollable and so always having to drive away hungry. His unexplainable allergy to certain sounds, reducing him to a quivering, sneezing, wreck every time someone played certain musical notes. His irrational fear of one day having an irrational fear. His confusion over the fact that, given that having an irrational fear was something which one could rationally fear, he was not sure that it was in fact irrational to fear it. Puma listened and tried to understand.

Above all, that which the two shared, indeed, that which had originally brought them together, was their

Arthur: An Actuarial Odyssey

common obsession with life extension. It was all Arthur now lived for. Puma had been structuring her daily life around life extension rules and principles for years. Arthur's adjustment did not come about overnight. Arthur had always loved a good steak, for instance. Such a meal would be unthinkable now. The first thing all new Healthier-than-Thou life-extenders did was to remove all dangerous items, such as sharp objects, from the household. The steak knives were the first to go. In fact, Arthur's entire way of living had been completely revolutionized both by Puma as well as by his new life-extension regiment.

Each morning at five he would wake. But not to his old alarm clock which had been slowly sending him to an early grave with its mind-shattering screech.

"Oh sure," his fellow life-extenders would tell him, "it'll wake you up. But at what cost? Each morning you were subjecting your nerves to a veritable torture chamber of shock waves."

Now, courtesy of the Healthier-than-Thou Life-Extenders Gift Shop he had bought a new "nerve-friendly, anti-sleep device." The device had a speaker and two mechanical arms.

Each morning at precisely five a.m., one mechanical arm would softly pull the covers from the bed, while the other gently nudged the pillow. Meanwhile, a soft voice, recorded to match the voice of the person's mother, would call out, "It's time to wakee-wake. It's time to

Arthur: An Actuarial Odyssey

experience another long and beautiful life-extension day." Arthur initially had some minor difficulties with the device's original factory settings and he spent a week or so going through some "very routine" psycho-therapy, after he woke the first few mornings to his mother pounding him in the gut, while trying to smother him with his pillow and screaming for him to "Get the hell out of bed, you lousy, lazy shit!"

Once awake he would brush his teeth and floss with his Healthier-than-Thou Life-Extenders Dental Kit. Following oral hygiene, Arthur would jump in the shower. Showering was a still-evolving concept with life-extenders. A great many dangers surrounded the ritual, most particularly slipping. Therefore, all Healthier-than-Thou life-extenders were counseled to continuously jump up and down while taking a shower on the theory that this would keep someone constantly on guard against slipping. Every time the neighbors would come up to complain they would find a dripping-wet Arthur standing in his robe. Confused and thinking they must have been mistaken, they generally left offering apologies.

After showering, Arthur stood before his closet admiring his collection of fire-retardant, polyester clothes. The Healthier-than-Thou Life-Extender's latest findings offered definitive proof that polyester beside one's skin offered the surest protection against aging. While this finding had initially resulted in the loss of nearly a third of their membership under the age of 40, this proved only a short-term loss.

Arthur: An Actuarial Odyssey

Arthur slipped into his polyester sweat pants and T-shirt, downed some o.j. and headed out for a jog. In fact, Healthier-than-Thou life extenders had made quite a reputation for themselves down at the gym with their innovative jogging routine. On the ingeniously counter-intuitive theory that nine out of ten jogging injuries occur in the stretching period, Healthier-than-Thou researchers recommended shortening the stretching exercises and, just to be safe, saving them for *after* the actual jogging.

So Arthur would start right into his "jogging" without risking injury in the warm-up. At the same time, Healthier-than-Thou jogging was not precisely what most people considered "jogging" per se. Again, fearing that running freely at a moderate pace could place a person at unnecessary risk, Healthier-than-Thou joggers would carefully walk out onto the track whereupon they would lay on their backs and simulate the motion of jogging by waving their arms and legs in the air. Healthier-than-Thou members found this to be every bit as demanding a workout as actually running about on one's feet. It was the case, however, that the one or two life extenders who had become particularly proficient in this exercise and gone on to enter actual competitive road races had not really done very well.

A half-hour of Healthier-than-Thou jogging had Arthur jumping back in the shower. However, after several anonymous complaints at the gym, Arthur was urged to take his showers back home. Knowing his kind to be far too advanced to ever be fully accepted by those

Arthur: An Actuarial Odyssey

from a mainstream society of normal life-span people, Arthur abided. Riding home on his tricycle, he'd pass Dirk's Donut Heaven, where he'd flirted with death on oh so many mornings before he'd been introduced to the life-extension way of living. Further along, he'd wave to the paperboy making his way on his death-defying bicycle. As Healthier-than-Thou life-extenders liked to say, "If God had meant for us to roll around on two wheels, than God would have made the crash helmet and not the derby the fashionable headwear of the early 20th century." Ah, the wisdom of those life-extending sages, Arthur would chuckle to himself as he rounded the corner home.

There in the kitchen Puma waited. She'd been up since five, as well. In keeping with the Healthier-than-Thou's fiercely anti-patriarchal philosophy, she had been waiting nearly an hour for Arthur to return and prepare her morning meal. She passed the time, sitting in the living room in her torn bath robe and watching "The Manly Man's Body-Builder Morning Stretch," while flipping through a stack of vintage *Playgirls*.

"I'll have those whole-wheat flapjacks ready in a sec' honeybun," Arthur assured, as he gave her a peck on the cheek.

Puma grunted and turned her attention back to Mr. July.

The Healthier-than-Thou Life-Extender's position on patriarchy was not a political statement. It was based on sound, irrefutable science. Researchers had discovered a

Arthur: An Actuarial Odyssey

clear link between the extension of a woman's life-span and her opportunity to live free of repressive, male-dominated, social conventions. To most effectively assure the protection of female life-extenders from a lifetime of such patriarchal attitudes, women were instructed to select those traits of men under patriarchy which they considered the most obnoxious and adopt them. The specific trait could change each month. This month, Puma had chosen the disagreeable, early morning, sexist pig.

In general, Arthur did not have a problem with this arrangement. However, he did find it difficult at times to continue stirring the pancake batter without spilling, when Puma would sneak up behind to pinch his behind and ask why he never served any sausage with the flapjacks in the morning.

After everything was ready, he would set things out on the table and call Puma in to eat.

"In-a-minute!" Puma would bark, with the words pushed together to form a single garbled sound.

Arthur waited patiently by the stove to keep Puma's flapjacks warm, as she urged on some bench pressing hunk on tv in the next room. "Oh yeah, just 3 more Jake. That's it oooone... twoooooo... oh yeah for me baby, that's... threeeeee!"

With that, she shut off the set and made her way to the kitchen. Burping and wiping some slobber from her cheek with the corner of her robe, Puma sat to eat. When actually eating—or, "devouring the nutrients of life"—

Arthur: An Actuarial Odyssey

Puma would drop the personality of a disagreeable, early morning, sexist pig and the two would politely discuss their plans for the day.

Arthur never knew from day-to-day what his new life would teach him. He spent the first few months of his extended-life experience in care-free splendor, living each moment as if it could not possibly be his last. Some days he would go to the zoo and just sit watching the animals or, as he wondered, were they, in fact, not watching him. Zoo officials eventually secured a restraining order for Arthur after his paranoia had apparently gotten the better of him. Convinced that several primates in the monkey house had set up the entire exhibit as some bizarre experiment to study human beings in their own habitat, he was certain that several monkeys swung about on ropes with cameras at the ready.

Arthur would thus purposely exhibit unusual human behaviors to coax the monkeys into snapping his picture as proof. He was eventually led away one day screaming at the monkeys, "You don't fool me for a minute! I've been on to you from the beginning! Go ahead take my picture! You didn't even build the place with enough light, you morons!"

Not long after this fiasco, seeking further excitement, Arthur dressed as a janitor and snuck into the county hospital to dust and mop, ingeniously passing himself off as an actual sanitation worker. Much to his chagrin, however, Arthur soon found that life as a hospital janitor could be brutally boring. When he first started posing as a

Arthur: An Actuarial Odyssey

janitor at the hospital he'd sought a challenging and rewarding opportunity to aid the sick and dying. After nearly six weeks on the job, while he could see some indirect comfort he was providing the infirmed, he still thought there must be more he could do, an even greater service he could provide. Arthur dreamed of delivering linen service not twice, but three times a day; of better utilizing his skills of cleaning, disinfecting, and de-sterilizing to bring about even greater comfort to those for whom he slaved.

It was late one night in a meeting of the hospital custodial union, local 198, that the answer came to Arthur—organize! Of course. The custodians had a union. The doctors, the nurses, all had unions. So who was without? That's right, the patients—the people—were not organized. They had no voice.

The People United, Can Never Be Medically Cheated! This would be their rallying cry. This would be their vision. Arthur set to work on this right away. Within a week the entire maternity ward was in revolt. They refused participation in any further Lamaze classes until receiving complete recognition for the Organization of Maternity Patients. On the fourth floor orthopedics unit, nurses were turned back by angry voices encased in plaster. The gastroenterology wing had become a war zone, as marauding bands of patients roamed the halls armed with enema bags. The movement had taken hold.

The impetus of a people in revolt could not be reversed by any force known to humanity. The hospital was nearly shut down twice. The state police were put on alert. A SWAT team was called off at the last moment when a standoff in the hospital cafeteria between enraged heart patients—backed by a newly-created paramilitary wing of liver disease patients—and hospital security was averted by word of official recognition by the nurses' union for the Organization of Revolutionary Orthopedic Patients.

This recognition, however, created tremendous strife between the nurses' union and the doctors' union who earlier had recognized the Orthopedic People's Organization as the true representatives of orthopedic patients. At the same time, there were major divisions within the custodians' union who, while siding with the doctors on the issue of orthopedic representation, sided with the nurses in support for the maternity wing's demand for the withholding of payment until the ugliness of a newborn could be determined.

Political strife throughout the hospital was now rampant and growing. Doctors, nurses, and custodians harried about in a mad rush to line up support from sympathetic patient's movements, while simultaneously moving to suppress those movements counter to their ideological leanings. The patients, meanwhile, were just as divided. In late August things came to a head, as all four factions threatened chaos and paralysis across the hospital. An arbitrator was called upon. In the balance lay future control over critical hospital operations. All three unions had a solid core of patient support behind them.

Arthur: An Actuarial Odyssey

There remained only one patient's movement yet to be co-opted. Those who got them, got control of the hospital.

They were a sly group; in some ways the most radical, in other ways, the most accommodating. They were the Terminally Ill People's Organization or TIPO. Originally beginning as a small, urban, guerrilla group taking refuge in a second floor linen closet, they'd gradually moved closer to the political center, but now they were preaching a syncretic doctrine of Gandhian Maoism. Their paramilitary unit was Passive Insurrection.

The doctors were the first to make overtures to TIPO. They offered to expand the number of research labs for the study of terminal illnesses. The nurses immediately countered this, declaring that the doctors couldn't deliver on their promise, and they offered to re-arrange the order of distributing meals so the terminally ill patients got their food first when it was still hot. This erupted in the nurses' faces as the John Birch Society of Schizophrenic Patients swiftly reminded the nurses of a similar promise made to them. The custodians union was quick to step in and offer TIPO direct funding for their treasury.

The arbitrator was stumped. He'd managed hundreds of disputes. This time things looked impossible. He entered a room with representatives from all the factions. For days they battled. Finally, much wearied and emotionally drained, the negotiators emerged from their cell with a solid agreement. The doctors' union, nurses' union, and custodians' union would resume their previous powers of influence and a new umbrella organization

Arthur: An Actuarial Odyssey

representing all of the hospital's patients, to be called People United in Sickness and Suffering, or PUSS, would be formed as an independent entity with powers and authority to work for the betterment of the patients as a whole. Arthur's work was done. The patients were organized. The hospital was once again a smooth operating medical machine.

Of course, not all of Arthur's days were quite so eventful and exciting. Arthur passed most of the time absorbing volumes of Healthier-than-Thou Life-Extension materials. He wanted to know as much as he could. He'd spend hour upon hour, afternoon after afternoon, browsing through the Healthier-than-Thou Reading Room. He could hardly wait to rush home each evening and share with Puma a new discovery or nugget of unquestioned truth for that day. Their life together was a carefree, blissful, happy period of unadulterated fun and joy.

One day, sitting alone in the reading room and leafing through the latest issue of the Healthier-than-Thou's monthly magazine, *Your Subscription For Life*—featuring the latest studies on "Swivel Chairs and Life-Extension: The Hidden Hazards"—Arthur's mind turned to thoughts of Puma.

Lately it seemed he had been thinking only of Puma. How his life had been transformed from the moment he first stumbled upon her. How their passion for life-extension had only brought them closer together. He knew what he had to do. He had to ask Puma to share her

Arthur: An Actuarial Odyssey

and his extended lives with one another. Puma found herself so excited by Arthur's unexpected proposal—Arthur had always maintained that the institution of marriage was a barbaric reification of a pretentious, decadent society—that she leaped into his arms screaming, "Yes, yes! A thousand times yes!" with horrified shoppers looking on, as Arthur fell back against the escalator rail.

Arthur: An Actuarial Odyssey

Chapter Seven

By that May the two had wed. It was a simple ceremony, involving a small circle of fellow Healthier-than-Thou life extenders. By late June, Puma was expecting and early that Spring little Ferdinand was born. Arthur's quest for a stable, middle-class, nuclear family of life-extenders had finally come to fruition. Arthur now needed to provide for his family and he set out to find gainful employment. His job search led him at first along a difficult path of short-lived, dead-end jobs.

One of Arthur's more brief career moves was a short stint in the motion picture industry. Arthur answered an ad in the local paper for "a producer/director/writer for low-budget documentary/public service films—no experience needed" and soon found himself in the director's chair on a movie set, overseeing the action.

Arthur considered his film work highly experimental. This particular project required a dedicated cast trained in the art of spontaneous improvisation, regardless of

Arthur: An Actuarial Odyssey

whether a performer had any actual role in the scene or not. Ironically enough, the story line focused on the character of Baxter Reflex, a young, up-and-coming film director. The film opened with Baxter Reflex having just shot the final scene of his epic-thriller "Yuppies from Hell." Suddenly, a soft voice called to him from the bushes.

"Well, Baxter," the voice rasped seductively, "I guess that's a wrap."

It wasn't the first time Baxter's bush had spoken to him, but there was something hauntingly titillating about the voice today. As was his habit, Baxter ignored the bush and sped away on a crowded city bus. While on the bus, however, Baxter had further thoughts.

"I wonder... oh no, that would hardly be possible."

Realizing half way into his thought that his voice had carried throughout the bus, Baxter tried playing off his little indiscretion by instinctively whipping out a harmonica, playing a few notes, and putting his words to melody, as if composing a song. Before he knew, it several people behind him joined in, singing the chorus. Now Baxter was really in trouble. If he didn't want to look like a complete idiot he would have to complete an entire stanza before coming to his stop. Uncanny improvisation pulled Baxter through.

That night, Baxter lay awake in his hammock thinking only of the bush. He couldn't sleep. Oh, maybe it was the cool night air, the droning tv in the next room, or maybe

Arthur: An Actuarial Odyssey

it was simply international strife. But no, Baxter knew better. It was the bush. He snuck out late that night and hailed a cab to head down and meet the bush. The bush hadn't moved.

"I guess you know why I'm here," Baxter called out as he approached.

The bush said nothing.

"I mean don't get the wrong idea—it's not cause I'm lonely or anything romantic like that."

The bush stared blankly.

"After all, you're a bush, I'm a human... things just wouldn't work out even if we wanted it to. Well, anyway I guess that's all I really had to say. Maybe I'd better just be going."

Baxter turned to leave.

"Baxter wait!" It was the bush.

Baxter stopped. "Yes?"

"I... I didn't want to have to tell you like this, but well... you know the budding spruce across the way there?"

Baxter peered into the dark night. "What of it?"

"Well... it's yours Baxter." And with that the bush broke down.

"I, I... I don't believe it. How? When?" Baxter pleaded.

Arthur: An Actuarial Odyssey

"Don't you remember that cast party? Well I guess you were pretty drunk. Anyway, you and a few others grabbed a bag of seeds from the greenery... Oh Baxter, I know you were young, uninhibited—well a few months later..."

Baxter was devastated.

"Oh my God!"

Suddenly it all came back to him. The party, the drinking, the carrying on. And the next morning waking up in a strange bed beside that empty bag of seeds!

"What have I done!?! What have I done!?!"

"CUT!"

The lights went up.

"I don't know Leon," Arthur said, turning to his assistant. "You're sure we haven't compromised too much to get an effective, responsible safe-sex film into the classroom."

"I'm telling you it's the only way these days," Leon assured.

Months later, his work—Horticultural High—was eviscerated by the critics and Arthur returned to the want ads. A string of waiter jobs went nowhere—especially with Arthur's constant critique of customers' menu choices and his annoying habit of guessing at what age a customer would die based on their selection. At one point, Arthur had actually worked his way up to a mid-level

Arthur: An Actuarial Odyssey

management position at a quite successful fast-food franchise. He had finally come to terms with the dearth of nutritional value in the food products he was promoting and had disciplined himself to stop visibly grimacing and grinding his teeth every time someone ordered the "Super Deluxe Cheeseburger Surprise." What ultimately broke Arthur was the sheer monotony of fast-food work, combined with growing doubts about his truly making a gastronomical difference.

Day after day he would arrive to open his Uncle Murray's Food-Fest franchise, desperately trying to convince himself of the value of his work to humanity. At one point, for example, Arthur was possessed with the thought of adding a new item to the Food-Fest menu. Recognizing that the traditional hamburger had long ago morphed into a variety of non-beef burger forms—the turkey burger, the veggie burger, the fish burger, and so on—Arther convinced himself that the public was ready for a radical new addition to the American diet. Thus, his inspiration, the seal burger.

He was told that for something this awesome he would have to run it by corporate back in New York. Thus, toting his experimental seal burger in his Food-Fest carry-out bag—complete with appropriate condiments—Arthur jetted off for New York to meet with the suites on the 66th floor in the company boardroom.

Having left in excited haste, Arthur arrived too late to change out of his Uncle Murray's Food-Fest uniform. Happily, Arthur felt this added a certain grandeur to his

Arthur: An Actuarial Odyssey

entrance. After introducing himself, he apologized for his formal attire and presented his seal burger for inspection. An audible hush fell over the corporate clones as he placed his creation in the center of the conference table. The board chair immediately notified his secretary to cancel his meetings for that day and lock elevator access to the 66th floor.

The board had never seen anything quite like it. They were keen to know if the competition knew anything about his daring experimentation with sea-life. Arthur explained that the streets were rife with rumors about this or that innovation from other chains, but that the market for seal within fast food eateries remained wide open.

Several traditionally-minded board clones were skeptical, saying that they'd built the company on hamburgers and, by God, hamburgers had been good enough for the public back in their day. Arthur was aware of the seismic shake-up that had followed the introduction of cheeseburgers in the late '60's. Heads had apparently rolled at the time, when the cheeseburger prototypes were met by widespread customer rebellion.

Only several years later, after careful market research revealed dire design flaws, did the board authorize placing the cheese between the hamburger and bun rather than on top of the bun. Arthur knew he was up against the legacy of such cataclysmic failures.

Several younger clones seemed quite taken by the notion of seal burgers. At one point a screaming match

Arthur: An Actuarial Odyssey

ensued between a younger and older clone, with the older clone accusing the younger one of completely misreading the so-called "revolution" in curly fries that in fact never materialized. The company had sunk a small fortune into the promotion of curly fries in the early stages of their development. While initial indications were positive, the public never completely abandoned their trusted, linear potato fry. The point remained a touchy one between younger and older board members.

Arthur was asked to say a few words on behalf of his seal burger. He suggested that there were several marketing advantages for the seal burger. Number one, from the standpoint of the public, no bones. Number two, from the standpoint of the company, no seal. In fact, the seal burger contained virtually no seal whatsoever and was, therefore, quite cost-effective to produce. While the hamburger also contained little actual beef, the seal burger was slathered in batter and after first hooking the customer, the seal content of the seal burger could easily be further reduced by increasing the batter content. This met with much approval. But the board wanted to know what the market research was showing.

Arthur explained that not all data was in. However, early results from focus groups in the Midwest had demonstrated high name recognition and a positive disposition, in general, toward the concept of a seal burger. Asked, for instance: Are you now or have you ever knowingly kept company with known seal burger eaters?—over 85% said they had and only 6% of the

Arthur: An Actuarial Odyssey

entire sample said they had not and never knowingly would. The board members were impressed. Arthur had done his homework. Still a few clones were skeptical. In the end, the board agreed to allow Arthur's local Uncle Murray Food-Fest franchise to make a limited trial run with seal burgers.

However, after only three months of poor sales, the trial run was abandoned and seal burgers were taken off the Uncle Murray Food-Fest menu. Arthur was despondent and did not speak for several weeks after this. Finally, convinced that his job was utterly lacking in any redeeming social value whatsoever and knowing his chances for advancement to be extremely limited— following the seal burger fiasco—Arthur lost hope. Vowing to force Uncle Murray's Food-Fest out of business rather than quit outright, so that he could still claim unemployment, Arthur went to work on his new plan.

First, he ordered a batch of new ad flyers which extended a special offer to "satanic worshipers with dribbling problems" in extra fine print. All that week the staff worked overtime wiping down tables and washing all the "666's" off the bathroom walls. Needless to say, Uncle Murray's regular customers were soon put off by the new customers' incessant chanting and occasional ritual sacrifices, while taking advantage of their special discounts. Before long, however, the volume of drooling, satanic worshipers had grown large enough to compensate for the loss of regular customers. In fact,

Arthur: An Actuarial Odyssey

Uncle Murray's Food-Fest was pulling in more money than ever. Arthur would have to move to Phase B.

He began to spend his nights stealing lawn ornaments and mailboxes from homes in the immediate vicinity of Uncle Murray's Food-Fest. He would take the stolen items back to Uncle Murray's and display them prominently inside and outside the restaurant. Irate homeowners would show up demanding the return of their ceramic Bambi or plastic lawn elf. Unable to account for the mysterious appearance of stolen items throughout the restaurant, management decided to turn the peculiar crime spree into a promotional gimmick. A free soft drink was offered with any meal to anyone who could find a piece of their property on the restaurant's premises. By the second week, Arthur's plan had completely backfired. Local residents were sneaking by the restaurant late at night and planting various personal items on the grounds to cash in the next day.

Arthur had enough. He set out to completely disrupt Uncle Murray's Food-Fest's supply network. Secretly accessing company computer accounts from home, Arthur managed to switch Uncle Murray's Food-Fest's supply orders with Bert's Adult Party Gift Center. As trucks full of sauerkraut and Uncle Murray's Magic Buns were unloaded at Bert's, an assortment of whips, manacles, and nipple clamps were delivered to satisfy Uncle Murray's famished customers.

Again, however, necessity being the mother of invention, Uncle Murray's management team went to

Arthur: An Actuarial Odyssey

work re-fashioning the menu. Uncle Murray's Food Fest soon became known as the place "where we combine fine food and a warm, inviting atmosphere, with just a touch of S and M for old-fashioned, family fun!" All agreed that the locally-run tv spots, featuring a leather-clad dominatrix tempting her shackled prey with an Uncle Murray Food-Fest Hamburger Treat, were done in a provocative, yet tasteful manner. Arthur nearly buckled. He had one last chance.

He made a few phone calls. Then, late one night he drove out to a desolate airport access road to meet some "associates" who—for a price—would agree to help carry out Arthur's scheme. Desperate and feeling himself to have no further options, in the dark hours of the night, Arthur cut his engine and rolled silently into the brush. He got out and approached the six men sitting in the back of a tan, rusted van by the roadside. Initially, Arthur balked when the men claimed the risk was too high and demanded more money upfront. After a brief, heated discussion both sides agreed to terms. Arthur crawled back into the thick brush and waited for the men to drive off. As their tail lights disappeared down the dark road, Arthur emerged with a sinister grin.

By that afternoon the full gruesomeness of the early dawn transaction began to play out. When the unemployed mime troupe who Arthur had hired arrived to terrorize Uncle Murray's Food-Fest customers, the fruits of Arthur's plan took little time to ripen. These mimes were good and they meant business—whether incessantly

Arthur: An Actuarial Odyssey

pulling on imaginary ropes, struggling to free themselves from invisible boxes, or leaning whimsically on non-existent countertops.

Distraught customers streamed from the dining area dazed and disoriented. After clearing out the restaurant with rote exhibitions of their maddening craft, the mime terrorists pursued the fleeing diners out into the parking lot. Parking imaginary cars, the relentless mimers now had customers swerving all over the pavement. In short order, the mimes' harrowing exploits proved exceedingly effective and they piled back into their tan and rusting van.

Arthur: An Actuarial Odyssey

Chapter Eight

Following his dismal failures in the bare-knuckled world of fast-food eateries, Arthur spent a month or so filling in as a gas station attendee around town before landing what would become his first real career break. There was an opening at Sparky's Improv and Grill. They were looking for a female impersonator with a soulful yet coquettish vibe and a smooth, sultry sound for a few light jazz numbers. Arthur dusted off his *Stormy Weather* 45 and headed off for an audition. He did his best with the melody, but once the manager saw Arthur's legs not one note more need be sung. He was hired on the spot to open that very night.

Sparky's could attract a pretty rough crowd. Arthur was warned to look out for himself. Opening night jitters aside, Arthur was at last confident that he had made a long-term career move to support his stable, middle-class, nuclear, life-extension family lifestyle. Little Ferdinand was now nearly two and Puma was dropping hints of wanting to have another little life-extender.

Yes, life was good. After so many years of searching, it seemed Arthur had at last found true happiness. He was

Arthur: An Actuarial Odyssey

at peace there up on the stage. His velvet voice drawing in a sea of nameless, faceless customers, his pulsating torso exposed to all as a steamy, lustful tease, Arthur performed; watching nights turning into mornings, weeks into months, and winters into summers. There on stage, Arthur was free; free at last, to truly let his hair down. Free to express feelings he never knew burned within; to please large hordes of men he had previously only known as friends and colleagues. As time wore on, however, the business' toll on Arthur became more and more evident.

Stumbling in at 4 or 5 in the morning, his spiked heels catching in the rug, his long, golden locks snaring a lampshade, as he quietly crept into bed beside a sleeping Puma, Arthur could no longer deny that his new vocation was beginning to effect his home life. He struggled to live a "normal" life off stage. However, trips to the grocery store soon became major media events, as autograph-hounds—recognizing Arthur from his poster-image which plastered the town, as well as, his many appearances on afternoon talk shows—would surround Arthur and his cart. He and Puma discussed their increasingly tattered lives many times. But the money was good and the two had grown accustomed to a certain lifestyle. So Arthur resolutely pushed on.

Still, as time went by, try as he might, Arthur knew a certain magic was missing which had been there in the early days of his cabaret career. Lately, Arthur was experiencing mood swings and depression. The slightest disruption could throw him off. He abruptly deserted the

Arthur: An Actuarial Odyssey

stage one night during a performance of "Steam Heat" when he learned from a patron—while sitting on his lap—that China was threatening to pull out of the Nuclear Non-Proliferation Treaty. To many, Arthur's behavior was unpredictable and irreverent. For Puma, however, Arthur's problems seemed much deeper. She saw Arthur as a highly complex and deeply confused psychopath. At any rate, Arthur muddled on. But three shows a night, six nights a week had their effect.

Increasingly, Arthur struggled to maintain his concentration. He would find himself at times sleepily drifting in and out. A bizarre dream world became an escape from his demanding reality. Arthur's dreams had an almost surreal quality to them. Relaxing backstage between shows one night, Arthur fell off to sleep; dreaming he was sitting in a movie theater beside Puma. He could hear the movie characters, yet their dialogue felt somehow forced.

"Where is the princess? What have you done with her?"

"Ha, you'd love to know that, wouldn't you? Then all the townspeople could dance naked in the streets up to their ankles in crocodile manure!"

Arthur fidgeted in his chair. He draped his left arm over the arm rest, slouched slightly, and drew his right hand behind his head, fondling his right ear with an extended ring finger and released a slow, audible moan.

"Try and sit still dear," Puma prodded.

Arthur: An Actuarial Odyssey

"But… can you believe this dialogue? And those costumes?"

Arthur's critique grew louder, inciting a bevy of movie-goers to suggest what he could do with his opinions, along with a very disgusted look of repulsion from the white man sitting in front of him.

"You see. You're making a nuisance of yourself. Now sit and enjoy the movie."

Arthur didn't know what it was. He just couldn't sit still. So he blew a kiss to his wife that was mistakenly received by a startled middle-aged man to his right, as his wife bent to scratch her left ankle, which she remembered, too late, was wooden. Arthur could still hear her screams, as he hit the pavement outside, and others groped about in the dark, attempting to remove a blood-gushing splinter.

The cool air felt soothing against Arthur's black, leather ski mask. He walked down the street toward a large building made entirely of masonry. He was about to cross the street for a better look when suddenly the Earth opened up, swallowing the entire structure. Arthur stood awestruck. He turned to remark upon the experience with others but there was no one in sight. He stood alone before the giant cavern in the center of Blaker Street.

Then, from out of nowhere, a figure materialized. It was Rabbi Finkelstein.

"Some hole," remarked the Rabbi.

Arthur: An Actuarial Odyssey

"Yeah, and—"

"Look!" The Rabbi pointed excitedly to another building. But as Arthur turned to look, the Rabbi shoved him into the hole. Arthur, stunned, continued to fall for what felt like hours, but turned out to be hundreds of minutes. When he finally landed, Arthur found himself at the wheel of an 1935 Packard, driving through a neighborhood littered with the bodies of dead chickens, each dressed as an insurance agent. Arthur pulled over and approached one of the dead chickens to check his briefcase.

What he found, astounded and astonished him. Beneath a file of actuarial charts, there were news clippings about an underground movement to "free the bipedal beasts," along with some kind of most wanted list with a bunch of human stick figures sketched in. Suddenly, Arthur heard sirens. He tried to hide, but it was too late. The chicken police were on to him. He raced through the streets, dodging a barrage of fertilized human embryos. But escape was futile. He was eventually brought down by two police chickens. They ambushed him, hiding behind a chicken-feed vending machine. Feathers flew and Arthur was taken into custody.

"I won't talk! Hear me, I won't talk!" Arthur cried.

"You'll talk. We chickens have ways of making you talk," assured an obscenely fat chicken officer down at police headquarters.

"What do you want from me? Why am I here?"

Arthur: An Actuarial Odyssey

"We know what you did. So just knock off the act." And he slapped Arthur across the face with a wing.

"I demand to see a lawyer! Where's my lawyer!?!"

The large chicken nodded to another chicken posted by the door who then left, returning a few minutes later with a very tall and lean lawyer chicken who strutted in with a briefcase.

"Don't worry Artie. This one's in the bag."

"Think so?"

"No sweat. Alright, who's the clown in charge around here?" the lawyer chicken demanded.

"The chief'll be down in a minute," replied the fat chicken officer.

"Well, I'm counting," said chicken lawyer, dramatically winking towards Arthur.

The chicken chief of justice burst into the room a short while later, appearing quite agitated.

"Where's my coffee? Where's my gavel? Who the hell are these guys?"

The lawyer chicken moved forward to present his card. "My name is—"

The fat chicken cop interrupted. "This here is the sick kook who stole all the ball bearings from the governor's lawnmower, sending his gardener headlong into the hedges."

Arthur: An Actuarial Odyssey

"Put 'em away for life!"

"What!?!"

"Well, can't say I didn't try," consoled the chicken lawyer, as Arthur was taken away to a large human being coop.

He remained there for months, surviving on a steady diet of toothpaste and baking soda. When he brushed his teeth, Arthur would disappear in a cloud of suds. A ragged assortment of inmates was there doing time alongside him. There was Tom, who always sat by himself in the corner. Nobody messed with Tom. No one really knew what he'd done. But it was rumored that the secret chicken police had caught him at home, alone, licking his fingers. The one they called Funny Man was thought less dangerous. But he was just as much the recluse as Tom. He'd been picked up a few weeks before Arthur for reportedly calling the President "a lipless wonder who didn't even know why he crossed the street."

Arthur himself was seen as a bit of an oddball. No one really knew why he'd landed behind bars. He didn't exactly know himself.

"What cha in fer?" they'd ask.

"Dunno. They say I tried to kill the governor's gardener."

Arthur could see they weren't impressed. Prison life proved rough on Arthur and he knew it was only a matter of time before he broke. One day in the work yard

Arthur: An Actuarial Odyssey

Arthur's boiling frustration finally surfaced. He and a few other humans had gathered by the basketball courts. The chicken guards did not like this. They tried to break it up. Arthur lashed out in rage. He was a madman, swinging wildly at chickens left and right. When all was said and done it took upwards of 40 to 45 dozen fertilized human embryos to subdue him. Arthur dripped of embryo from head to toe, as they led him away cursing and swearing.

The chicken warden threw Arthur into solitary confinement. There he stayed for weeks on end. In the fifth week the warden got a letter. It was the chicken President. The nation's chicken scientists had been experimenting with a highly classified top secret drug designed to curb head bobbing while walking. As yet untested, a guinea pig was needed. Arthur was their man.

The chicken guards moved him from his solitary cell back into the general population, never letting on to what they had planned. Arthur was still irate, but, for a time, more cooperative. The chicken guards secretly snuck the drug into Arthur's food. After dinner, the warden summoned Arthur to his office. The warden looked him over, as Arthur cooly sauntered into the room.

"Feeling okay?" the warden asked.

"What's it to you?" Arthur blurted back.

"Okay tough guy, we don't have to talk. I just wanna see you walk."

"What?"

Arthur: An Actuarial Odyssey

A chicken guard moved forward. "You heard him. Walk!" He pushed Arthur who stumbled at first, before continuing across the room, his head steady, the epitome of unbobbiness.

"Impressive, very impressive," the warden commended. "Now I'm gonna make a deal with you. Walk across the room again. And this time, if you can bob your head up and down, I will grant you your release."

"What!?! You want me to walk like a chicken?" an incredulous Arthur replied.

"Just do it!"

Arthur began across the room, but try as he might, he could not bring his head to bob up and down.

"I... I, I don't understand. I can't... I mean my head won't—"

"You can't do it can you!?!" The chicken warden was euphoric. "Call the President! Success at last!"

"I don't understand," Arthur mouthed.

"Never mind, never mind. This is a great day for chickens everywhere. I grant you your unconditional release, even *without* head bobbing! Life as we know it will never be the same. No more seeing the world as a blur. No more viewing everything as if standing on the deck of a ship! You've helped free all the chickens of the world! We are grateful. You sir... are free."

Arthur: An Actuarial Odyssey

The chickens liberated Arthur just as he woke in his dressing room in a cold sweat. Arthur could feel himself being pulled deeper and deeper into this fantasy dream world. He sensed his safe, suburban life crumbling around him. His cabaret career, his nuclear family, his dedication to life-extension—it was all slipping from his grasp. The true depths of his despair at last hit home one evening, sitting in the unnatural glow of the family artificial fire beside Puma.

Arthur had just finished reading little Ferdinand his favorite Life-Extension-sanctioned bedtime story, "The Little Engine that Couldn't and Never Had Any Business Trying in the First Place." This was a delightful tale for children of all ages, providing an important lesson about the harmful effects of over-exertion. No little life-extender could grow up without the haunting image of the Little Engine succumbing to cardiac arrest, just as it reached the hilltop—having been urged on by some primordial, macho dogma—and sailing headlong down the other side to a twisted, ugly, fiery death.

Arthur and Puma sat silently listening to the contrived crackle of the smoldering artificial log. Just then, there was a scratch at the door. It was Ulysses, their faithful beagle. Ulysses was by nature a playful, happy dog. But this evening he did not seem himself. He acted cold and withdrawn. Ulysses had never been especially moody before. Puma investigated. As it turned out, there truly was something different about Ulysses this night. He

Arthur: An Actuarial Odyssey

wore a brand new red and yellow collar. But neither Puma nor Arthur could recall any such collar.

Arthur removed the collar to further inspect. There was something written on the inside. "For a wonderful dog and loving companion—the Jones Family." Arthur was dumb struck. He fell back against the couch in shock. Ulysses, their seemingly faithful and trusted family pet, had been sneaking out on weekends to be with another family.

Arthur broke down, asking himself over and over how he'd missed the signs. Always so excited to be let out on Friday evenings. Always so withdrawn and tired when he dragged himself back in Monday mornings. That now understandable awkwardness the evening that the Jones family had dropped by for coffee, as they and Ulysses shared hidden glances. Arthur didn't know what to do. He could no longer walk Ulysses in public as, by now, surely all the other dogs in the neighborhood were on to the situation. They wouldn't *say* anything, but with those mocking sniffs and markings, Arthur knew what was being thought behind his back about his being two-timed by old, trustworthy Ulysses. How naive he had been.

Arthur thought back to the first day they brought Ulysses into their home. The happy, bouncing pup brought joy and happiness into their lives. He remembered the time Ulysses threw himself in the path of a truck to save little Ferdinand. Arthur had stayed by Ulysses' animal hospital bedside every night until he was well enough to go home. They had grown to be a family.

Arthur: An Actuarial Odyssey

But now… now with this unspeakable infidelity, Ulysses had broken that special bond, he had ripped the hearth from a young nuclear family's warm home.

There's a line all dogs instinctively know not to cross. Ulysses had gone too far. He knew what had to be done. He took back the shiny collar from Arthur between his teeth, gave one last mournful glance about the happy nuclear family's home that he had so selfishly destroyed and sadly waddled out the doggy door never to return.

This was too much for Arthur—the final straw as it were. He told Puma that the two had to talk. Lately he felt his life to be sailing aimlessly. When he'd first come across the life-extension way of life he had thought, "Yes, this is the answer." Now, Arthur confessed, he was no longer convinced. To Puma's ears this was plain blasphemy. She screamed for him to stop. When he begged her to understand, she ran to the bookshelf and began reading from *The Healthier-than-Thou Book of Eternity*.

"Please Puma, you must listen."

But Puma just kept reading aloud over his pleadings.

Arthur tried to make Puma understand how he recognized now that his whole life-extension fetish had been nothing more than a veiled effort to avoid confronting his true calling—to sell life insurance and, for this, first to search for the meaning and purpose of life so as to better know how to insure it. His words were futile.

Arthur: An Actuarial Odyssey

He saw now that Puma could not be rescued from her soothing, safe, and insulated, life-extension world. If his search was to continue it would have to continue—at least for now—without Puma and little Ferdinand. His fragile, suburban, dream world had collapsed like a house of cards.

Arthur: An Actuarial Odyssey

Chapter Nine

To begin afresh, Arthur decided to spend some time communing with nature. It would be just he and the elements, as Arthur solemnly turned his back on civilization. He would make the ferocious wilds his home, living off the land and searching for answers, as he competed with untamed beasts and vermin for his daily meal. It was thus, that he set out to hitch a ride out of town. There, standing by the roadside, his velvet duffel bag slung over his shoulder, Arthur at last felt he was free and truly alive. He was free to explore the frontiers he had earlier abandoned and free to boldly go forward to wherever his lonely queries led.

After an extended but fiercely confident period of waiting by the roadside, a car pulled over. Arthur got in. It was a dentist from Sioux Falls. He asked where Arthur was headed.

Arthur just pointed vaguely down the desolate stretch of highway and replied, "When I am there I will not know. When I have been there… when my having been there results in my knowing that I *was* there—and by that I mean actually *there*—then I will be there. Even though, technically, I will have been there and left by the time I realize I am there."

The two continued on in silence.

Reaching the forest's edge, Arthur and the dentist bid farewell. One final look back at civilization and Arthur threw back his head, let out a haughty laugh, and made his way into his new woodland home. He wandered directionless for days down untrod paths, through thick forest, past the dark night's savage creatures. Until this point, Arthur had only *read* of "trudging" in magazines, now he was actually out confronting the wild, pushing relentlessly deeper and deeper into the vast and foreboding world of nature as it truly was.

This was no picture book, Arthur thought to himself, smirking as he spied a raccoon relieving itself by a tree. No this was the unvarnished, ugly reality of the feral forestland. This was a world without grocery stores or movie theaters or recycling bins. Out here it would be just him and all the other animals of prey sharing one humongous eatery, entertainment center, and bathroom—all rolled into one.

A hawk circled above as Arthur crossed a raging river, hip-deep in the waters turgid rush. He held his dry duffel bag overhead and let out a second haughty laugh.

Arthur: An Actuarial Odyssey

"Hah!" Arthur cried, "No longer a slave shackled to a life of modern conveniences! I am as free as you Mr. Hawk! Yes, you and I are as one! Aha, Ha! Ha! Ha!"

Across the river, Arthur collapsed on the bank and the hawk made its move. In the blink of an eye, the hawk dove and made off with Arthur's last Happy Burger.

"Ha! Slave!" Arthur shouted at the hawk, licking Happy Burger Sauce from its beak.

Not four hours into his grueling survival-of-the-fittest contest and Arthur's provisions were nearly spent. He would have to truly rough it. From here on Arthur would live on a diet of nuts and berries. He imagined eventually he would be able to construct a few crude weapons and perhaps hunt down some wild beasts for special occasions. Days went by. Arthur pushed further and further into the unforgiving wilderness.

There were times—Arthur had to admit—when he felt as though he could not go on; that his energies were at their limit; that, alas, he simply must turn back. But from somewhere deep inside, from a reservoir of raw guts and courage which seems, somehow, to naturally reside within all *real* men like Arthur, a voice would call to him.

"You can't turn back now," the voice would admonish. "You don't know the way."

So Arthur trudged on, steeled with a kind of primordial confidence to tame this ferocious land and find what he was searching for.

Arthur: An Actuarial Odyssey

On day five, weak and having nearly exhausted his supply of Evian spring water, Arthur stumbled upon an abandoned cabin beside a small pond miles from the nearest sign of human civilization. He approached cautiously and first knocked in case someone—or *some thing*—might be inside. No answer. He scraped a layer of crusty dirt from a window and peered inside. The room lay in ruins, decayed and decrepit. The cabin itself—dilapidated inside and out—seemed to have been abandoned for years, maybe decades.

This, thought Arthur, would be the perfect spot for unbridled and undisturbed reflection upon human existence. To begin, he would need to force his way into the cabin. He grabbed a large stone and rushed madly at the cabin's heavy door. It did not budge. He grabbed an even larger stone and rushed even more madly again bursting upon the door. Nothing. Arthur and the stone fell in a pile on the front step.

Arthur had to think. He knew that he needed to push his mind beyond mere conventional deliberation. "How would a wild beast of the forest enter the cabin?" he thought to himself. But try as he might to become one with the thinking of a feral woodland creature, Arthur could not wipe from his mind the image of Mr. Bear heading down to the hardware store to ask Mr. Possum to cut him a key. He circled the cabin feeling his way for another entry point. He climbed onto the roof. It was a veritable fortress. He broke a window but the opening was too small for his frame. He'd have to eat a lot fewer berries to be going in and out that window every day.

Finally, Arthur broke down. After all, all men—even men of unusual bravery and sheer heartiness, such as Arthur—have their breaking point. This was his. Nature's unrelenting torment had shaken his resolve. He became a wild man, grabbing a spoon from his duffel bag and ferociously stabbing the cabin door. In mid-mayhem, Arthur lost his footing and, stumbling backwards, he tripped over the welcome mat, dislodging a stashed key. It did not take him long to find his way into the cabin after this. Crossing the threshold, Arthur complimented himself on his innate capacity to channel the primitive instincts of an animal living beyond captivity which had led to his discovery of the key.

He tossed his duffel bag in a corner and surveyed the wreckage he had wandered into. The main room was little more than a well-ordered assortment of filth and grime. A few pieces of furniture lay randomly scattered about. The cabin's rotted condition and unseemly appearance made it clear that, not only had it been a great while since anyone had lived here, but that that person's sense of decorating and basic color schemes could not have been more atrocious. Arthur was physically sickened by how badly the sofa clashed with the love seat. The wall paper and minimal natural lighting cried out for the end table to be moved away from the far wall and nearer to the brick fireplace.

Arthur: An Actuarial Odyssey

The kitchen contained a sink, a counter, and a wood-burning stove. All were old and worn, but functional. Again, however, the utensils drawer was almost a crime scene and the condition of the spice rack very nearly drove Arthur from the cabin. If Arthur was going to rough it, it was apparently going to be without nutmeg. Arthur cursed and turned back to the rest of the cabin. There was a bucket by the door to carry water from a nearby well.

Arthur pictured himself deep in thought, traipsing about with pails of water, no longer a prisoner of life's stultifying modern conveniences—the crushing weight of indoor plumbing having been lifted from his chest. He looked out the broken window and heartily screamed, "At last! My soul is free!" before starting to tidy up—first, separating the soup spoons from the tea spoons.

As he reached for a twisted spatula, a flat, plain object on a crooked table in the kitchen corner caught his eye. It was a small notebook; a crude diary of some kind. The first page was dated "February 6, 1977." Intrigued, Arthur began reading.

> *"Tuesday, February 6, 1977. Ten days we have journeyed through thicket and forest. We began as five and now we are two; Murray and I. CURSED BE THE GODS WHOSE WICKEDNESS BEMOANS OUR WRETCHED—"*

Arthur: An Actuarial Odyssey

Arthur skipped ahead.

Thursday, March 11, 1977. Today I captured a flower and brought it back to the cabin. I call it Daisy and here it lies on the table. Sad, quiet, lonely, desperate flower—mocking me with its sarcastic stare. Oh, this flower is clever. It thinks I can't understand. It thinks I'm some imbecile... Well, I'm no imbecile! I SAY I'M NO IMBECILE!

Monday, March 15, 1977. We buried the flower by the spring. Murray now fears that the ghost of the flower will return to haunt us. He has strung a necklace of flowerpots around his neck to protect himself from the evil flower spirits. He made one for me which I refuse to wear. He calls me a fool. But I said I didn't think that meant much coming from someone wearing a flowerpot necklace. He wanted to chase after me, but didn't dare, for fear of upsetting the flowerpots.

Tuesday, March 16, 1977. After a harrowing, torturous night I too am now wearing a flowerpot necklace. At 2 in the morning I was jolted from sleep by the image of a dandelion attacking me with a meat cleaver. Behind it came a geranium with a chain saw. I tried to run but my feet were buried up to my ankles in flower pots. I tried to call out to Murray sleeping peacefully with the

Arthur: An Actuarial Odyssey

flowerpots around his neck, but I had no voice. In a panic... I fell unconscious.

When I came around I ran outside to check the spot where we had buried Daisy. Horror stricken, I found that the grave had been dug up! Suddenly, an army of flowers appeared. I was knocked from my feet. As I desperately crawled toward the cabin door, the flower militia advanced on me. I closed my eyes and screamed! Next thing I knew I woke in my bed in a cold sweat, as Murray pleaded with me to wear the flowerpot necklace he had crafted for me.

Friday, April 20, 1977. After a heated argument, Murray and I are no longer speaking. It seems that I accidentally severed his right arm, while stringing up some seasonal Christmas lights. Though I offered to help with the tourniquet, he would have nothing to do with me. In fact, the entire incident is really just a huge misunderstanding, which I assured Murray the two of us would look back on one day and laugh and laugh. It all began when I got my dates mixed up. Mistaking April 25th for December 25th (this is the part I am counting on for most of the laughs in a few years), I joyously began putting up Christmas lights.

At the time, Murray was out collecting firewood. On returning, the first thing to catch his eye was the tree. Then he saw me up on the

Arthur: An Actuarial Odyssey

ladder with the lights. "Ho! Ho! Ho!" I said to get him into the Christmas spirit. "What the hell are you doing?" said mean old Murray Scrooge. "Putting up the Christmas lights. What does it look like?" I said. "Christmas? What the hell are you talking about. It's not even—" at which point he brushed the tree which fell over, catching the string of lights, which pulled the ladder and knocked him over, with myself and the ladder landing on top of him, crushing one of his two then functioning arms.

Tuesday, April 24, 1977. Murray has adopted a very poor attitude toward his recovery. He's taken to nicknaming me Satan and hurling small pieces of furniture in my direction when I try to help him. I fear Murray may yet harbor some lingering resentment.

Thursday, May 26, 1977. Murray ate with me at the table for the first time in a month. Slowly he is coming to accept the new challenges life has handed him. He suggested we try to go fishing tomorrow out on the pond. I am encouraged by Murray's new-found zest for life.

Friday, May 27, 1977. Murray's new-found zest for life turned out to be a cheap ploy to get me out on the water where he could pummel me with an oar. Just as my back was turned, Murray struck. Fortunately, only able to grasp the oar with a single arm, the weight of the oar proved

Arthur: An Actuarial Odyssey

too much and pulled him backwards over the side of the boat, as he swung it over his head to strike. Instinctively, I dove in to rescue him. However, with my foot caught in the seat I inadvertently flipped the boat over, smashing a desperately flailing Murray in the head. I pulled his limp body to shore and brought him around, but again he blames me for his troubles.

Saturday, June 5, 1977. I woke today to find Murray and all his things gone. He left a note which was far too obscene to reprint here. Sufficed to say, Murray was not a particularly forgiving individual who possessed a rich and colorful imagination when it came to uses of body parts and bodily functions along with close relatives and livestock. So now I must go it alone. Now I must carry on as the lonely hunter. We set out for this forsaken woodland to live our lives as free as the animals whom we came to call our neighbors so that we could explore big questions. Now I alone remain to ponder the meaning of it all. Well, if I must carry on the search alone so be it—this is my calling.

Several years were missing from the diary at this point. It did not pick up again until October 1985.

Arthur: An Actuarial Odyssey

October 11, 1985. It has taken nearly a decade, but at last I have been able to outline a plan of action for discovering deep meaning and purpose. First, I must sit somewhere very quiet and think. Second, I must carry with me a pencil and pad of paper at all times—ever alert to the possibility of encountering ultimate understanding at any time. Third, I must go for long walks in the forest with a very serene and studious expression on my face so that, should ultimate truth see me, it will recognize that I am looking for it. Lastly, I must sleep with a pot of coffee at the ready to heat up on the stove, so that, should ultimate purpose visit me in the night, I won't be all groggy and miss an important point.

October 12, 1985. Spent all day sitting. Forgot to think. Will try again tomorrow.

October 15, 1985. Spent day walking in forest with a serene and studious look. I spotted two chipmunks by a tree with even more serene and studious expressions than mine. Fearing ultimate truth may reach them before seeing me, I re-doubled my efforts and devised an even more serene and serious look. Turned out the joke was on me as I had inadvertently caught the chipmunks relieving themselves. For the rest of the afternoon all the animals of the forest leaped from my path in apparent fright.

Arthur: An Actuarial Odyssey

October 29, 1985. Day-by-day I grow more despondent. My knees are weak from sitting. My pencils are brittle from little use. The nerves in my cheeks are completely numb from walking about with such a serene and studious look. How much longer I can go on I do not know. And yet, I must. Tomorrow I have a big day planned. For the first time ever I will actually combine activities. I will walk for a long time in the forest with a serene and studious look and then find a quiet spot to sit and think. This could be big.

Reading on, it seemed to Arthur that the search was growing futile. Then, finally, in the dead of winter. He found it.

February 2, 1988. At last! At long last... I have discovered deep meaning and purpose! Much like a bolt of lightning, it came to me as I lay in my boat adrift on the pond, contemplating the universe, a humming bird nearby, fluttering above a tree branch, swaying in the breeze. A oneness overcame me. A oneness and yet more than this. I would describe it as almost an everythingness as I felt myself, for the first time in my life—for the first time in my woefully tedious and uneventful 46 years—I felt myself in complete connection with the world around me.

Arthur: An Actuarial Odyssey

It was as if my mortal soul had been spirited away, lifted from the emptiness of its imprisoned material existence and allowed to soar the heights of a world majestically removed from the sterile, grinding, human sinkhole of modern society. I became the humming bird, fluttering above a tree branch, swaying in the breeze. I became the tree branch, swaying in the breeze. I became the breeze. Then, perhaps for only half a second, I became me becoming a humming bird, fluttering above a tree branch, swaying in the breeze. But before I could become me becoming me becoming a humming bird, fluttering above a tree branch, swaying in the breeze, I heard the voice of someone arriving at the cabin. It was the cable man!

Finally, after months of waiting, the magical world of cable tv was opened up to me. And it was then that I was at last able to find true meaning and purpose. I hadn't been surfing long before I found it. Channels 66 and 68—our local home shopping channels. I sat before the television's radiant glow, utterly in awe. Here, laid out before me for my instantaneous consumption, was every conceivable device of human creation. From the comfort of my own desolate cabin, it was possible to buy literally anything. And the sales pitches were so polished and so professional that I found myself fighting

Arthur: An Actuarial Odyssey

the urge to buy items I never otherwise could possibly have considered—a slightly used oboe, a toaster/vacuum cleaner combination appliance, a one-time only liquidation sale on the sperm of near-Nobel Prize winners. My searching is over. I have found true happiness.

I have found the ultimate purpose of human existence. So caught up in the monotony of our everyday lives, we are unable to see it. Out here, in the fresh air, at one with nature, it all becomes much more clear. The purpose of life is to buy stuff. The more one buys the more genuine our fulfillment. The more expensive the stuff one buys the more gratified are we. The more one—Oh my God! Oh my God! An overstock of genuine mink men's house slippers with deerskin lining! Only 500 left! Gotta go... gotta...

Arthur threw the diary down in disgust. Another innocent seeker slyly duped by a clever consumer society's sleekly packaged campaign to derail his earnest quest. Substituting true meaning for its false Gucci idols and Madison Avenue icons, the carnivores of conspicuous consumption had again snared their unsuspecting prey. Arthur had seen it before. No doubt this one had bought his third, special order pearl necklace and matching handbag with the option of monthly payments before he even knew what hit him.

Arthur: An Actuarial Odyssey

"Hah!" Arthur thought to himself, "Thoreau had it so easy in his day!"

The Winter days passed slowly as Arthur wrestled with the challenges of adjusting to his new rugged, survival-of-the-fittest lifestyle. In his first month he was able to devote precious little time to actually contemplating the meaning and purpose of life and spent most of his energies collecting berries and fending off nature's many murderous creatures whose hot breath Arthur felt, as they stalked his cabin day and night, awaiting an inadvertent slip, anticipating that fatal, careless moment.

One close call came in only his third day at the cabin. He had stepped out back to regain the instinctual hunting skills that modern society had robbed him of. He was gathering material to build a primitive, yet deadly accurate butterfly net, when from out of nowhere the savage beast pounced.

Arthur first caught sight of the wild animal less than 20 yards away. Everything happened with lightning speed. It was a blur. At first, he thought perhaps it was a crazed elk charging in a manic rampage, as Arthur assumed must happen out here in the lonely forest where Man and Beast are equals in a merciless battle of survival. Without time to think, he pivoted off his right foot and—in a single motion—he snatched a stone from the ground and contorted his cougar-like physique to hurl the weapon in pure defense. In his haste, however, Arthur lost his

Arthur: An Actuarial Odyssey

balance, tumbling backwards into the pond and releasing the stone wildly into the air.

This, nonetheless, startled the wild beast which, on second glance, was less a crazed elk and more a highly volatile and possibly carnivorous beaver, sending it off in stark terror. Arthur lay on his back in the muddy water, his butterfly net a tangled mess. Looking up into the sky he let out an exaggeratedly loud and haughty laugh.

"Hah! So this is how you test a man's steel, eh!?! Well, you'll have to do better than that! That's right, a lot better than that! Aha! Hah! Hah!"

Arthur now knew what he was up against and he took special care never to let his guard down for even a single second. His first month's acclimation could not have gone better. He'd found a bountiful supply of nuts and berries not far from the cabin. He'd learned to live at peace alongside his merciless neighbors of prey. In fact, he felt he'd gained a grudging respect from even the animal kingdom's most vicious hunters. They'd grown accustomed to seeing his self-confident, swaggering style as he roamed the forest collecting nuts and berries or silently crept about the underbrush with his butterfly net at the ready.

Of course, whenever he'd capture a butterfly he would immediately set it free. Not as an act of mercy. No, out here, Arthur knew, sentiment had no place—not in this cold and bloodthirsty world of kill or be killed. His only purpose in capturing butterflies was to perfect his predatory skills. He wanted to think like a beast of the forest. He wanted to tap into the primitive mind of his prey. So while hunting, for instance, he channeled the primordial consciousness of his butterfly foe.

"What would I do if someone was coming after me with a big stick with a net on it?" Arthur thought to himself. "I would dive up—no down. Maybe to the left. No, wait! I'd build anti-butterfly net devices."

Arthur now lay awake nights imagining what ingenious defensive weaponry the butterflies were working on. Days passed. It seemed almost as if the butterflies were baiting Arthur, as they continued to rely only upon the primitive techniques of diving up and diving down. Arthur sensed that they were planning something big. He didn't know what. But, as he lay awake nights, he couldn't help thinking that it was pretty quiet out there—too quiet. He started taking extra precautions when going out. He changed his schedule, collecting berries and then nuts instead of nuts and then berries. Eventually, the stress of the waiting game grew too great.

One night, the deafening silence became too loud. Arthur ran hysterically into the woods, cursing the butterfly conspirators. Then, that night, Arthur made peace with the butterflies. From that time forward he vowed to put an end to the war between he and they. No more would Arthur stalk the woods with the feared butterfly net, his cruel instrument of terror. They then would desist with their terrible retaliatory schemes.

Arthur: An Actuarial Odyssey

All in all, Arthur's first month of survival in the wilds went well. He'd grown accustomed to his new Spartan lifestyle. Each morning he woke to the sounds and smells of nature also waking. He took his bowl from the cupboard and prepared a hearty breakfast of nuts and berries. Then, as the sun made its way over the horizon, he would set out on a brisk and invigorating walk. This was the time of day Arthur most cherished. The birds chirped their good morning. The squirrels scurried past. And the morning dew tickled his feet.

"How?" Arthur would think at such moments, "How, could I have lived so sterile an existence lo' these many years, locked away in my cocoon of modern inventions?" No, there was no morning paper waiting on the front step of nature's door, Arthur thought.

By mid-afternoon, Arthur would return to the cabin for a hearty lunch of nuts and berries. Yes, this was a simple life. And Arthur had sense that out here—having left his castrated inhibitions back at the forest's edge—he would at last find some answers. He split his time in the afternoon between hunting and gathering and long, quiet periods of lying on his back in various places around the cabin deep in thought. After a rough start, Arthur's thoughts grew profound and meaningful, though contemplation did not come easily to Arthur at first. In the beginning, he tried lying on his stomach and not his back. But this was no good. His thoughts became shallow and infantile. Lying on his side, left him empty and slightly nauseas. It was in the third week that Arthur

Arthur: An Actuarial Odyssey

began to first perfect serious-minded contemplation while lying on his back.

Often, Arthur would conclude an afternoon's contemplation with a moment or two on his stomach. At first, this was nothing more than harmless fun after a hard day's thinking. Soon, however, lying on his stomach became like a drug to Arthur, an escape from the demanding world of heavy thoughts and deep rumination. He could feel himself being pulled into the sick, fantasy world of the stomach-layers. He fought the powerful urges with a fearsome resolve. One night, having tied himself down lying on his back, he woke to find that the straps had been ripped free and he was again frolicking uncontrollably on his stomach.

Though it was touch-and-go for a while, after a month's time, through sheer Man-of-the-wild will-power, Arthur had finally conquered the urges and could again confidently lie on his back. Arthur well understood that lying on his stomach was but one of many temptations that forces greater than he would throw in his path to thwart him from his mission. For this, Arthur was prepared.

Evenings were testaments to life's simple pleasures. As the sun set over the forest's edge, Arthur would sit to enjoy a hearty dinner of nuts and berries. At first, Arthur feared the monotony of meals may prove difficult. But—as Arthur came to convince himself—for any true woodsman each berry had its own flavor, each nut a distinct crunch. Thus, he knew that if he ate enough of these, eventually he would find some that he actually liked. Following the evening meal, Arthur would relax in a hammock he'd hung out behind the cabin.

There, under the stars, Arthur would gaze up into the heavens in wonderment, before drifting off to sleep to begin his daily cycle of discovery and awakenings once more. His was a true life of introspection, Arthur thought to himself. His was a world whose only limit would be the human imagination. His was a serenity known only to the courageous few who stray from the luxuries of modern living and seek out a life without rules, an existence undisturbed by the enslaving creature comforts of consumption, carnival, and cravings.

He'd been living off the land for nearly three months when the first hints of Winter came licking at the cabin door. Arthur collected extra nuts and berries for the harsh months ahead. He stocked up on branches and logs to keep a fire burning. It was going to take more than a stiff, Arctic breeze or blinding blizzard to pry Arthur from his quest. So the leaves turned colors and drifted to the ground, the air chilled the nights, and the creatures of the forest cowardly retreated to their wintry dens. All the while, Arthur's contemplative resolve did not wane.

Arthur: An Actuarial Odyssey

Chapter Ten

The long, winter months offered challenges beyond simply surviving the elements. Living alone in the desolate world of nature, void of human contact, there remained the very real danger of slowly going mad—in technical terms, cabin fever. Arthur, keenly aware of this peril, took meticulous care to watch for early signs of madness. For the most part, he maintained an even keel. Brisk walks, regular meals, and a developing relationship with a nearby family of beavers kept Arthur's keen mind focused. One day, however, while in his cabin staring blankly at the ceiling, Arthur could swear he heard voices. The words were jumbled, practically unrecognizable at first. But they seemed to almost be calling to him. Over time, the voices strengthened and even grew defiant—erupting into a steady, thunderous chant. Arthur lay confused.

He tried to block out the voices. He began singing himself as loudly as he could to drown out the incessant racket. Impulsively, he found himself leaping about the cabin, divining a spontaneous, modern dance. The sounds of his lively singing carried off into the woodland.

Arthur: An Actuarial Odyssey

"Fame! I'm gonna live forever! Baby remember myyyy name! Remember... remember..."

But it was no good. The choral chanting grew only louder. And so his singing likewise grew all the louder.

"I'M GONNA MAKE IT TO HEAVEN—"

The chanters' words became yet more loud and now more clear. Arthur's singing was now more scream than song. And his dancing also crescendoed to a feverish pitch.

"I'M GONNA LEARN HOW TO FLY!"

The chanting seeped through the cabin walls. "Free the Trees! Free the Trees!"

"FAME! I'M GONNA LIVE FOREVER!"

The chanting engulfed the cabin. "Stop the Chainsaws of Death! Preserve Our Woodlands!"

"I'M GONNA MAKE IT TO HEAVEN..."

"Rapacious Corporate Greed Stops Here! Free the Trees!"

Arthur, his singing and dancing having reached a climactic zenith, felt the rhythmic chanting fill his head. He burst out the cabin door, kicking high into the air and leaping about in frenzied dance.

"FAME! BABY REMEMBER MYYYY NAME."

Suddenly, all chanting stopped. Arthur froze after completing a full pirouette, his head cocked to the right

Arthur: An Actuarial Odyssey

and his arms stretching out to both sides. For a moment, a still quietude filled the forest. Arthur looked up. There, chained to a nearby grove of pine trees, was a small band of militant, environmental activists. Arthur remembered having read of such people in a recent *Reader's Digest* exposé. The article cautioned that these were unpredictable and easily excitable zealots with whom one must exercise extreme caution.

Arthur composed himself. He was uncertain how environmental activists might interpret his song and interpretive dance. He gingerly strolled over to the pine trees.

"Hi, my name is Arthur. I live in the cabin across the way. I couldn't help overhearing your screams of indignation."

"And what of it? Who are you? Some sadistic, corporate scout—sent to map the next area of rape and plunder?"

"No, no... I'm just an insurance salesman."

Before the hearty band of environmental activists could begin to fully fathom the horror of having chained themselves to trees in a desolate stretch of forestland with an insurance salesman, Arthur explained how he was on sabbatical in search for the ultimate meaning and purpose of life.

Arthur: An Actuarial Odyssey

"I have read of your struggle in a modern American periodical which keeps track of contemporary, social trends and movements," Arthur assured.

"And so you are with us my friend?"

"Well, I suppose I'm a bit of a fence-sitter." Arthur bit his tongue the second the words fell from his mouth.

"Fence!?! You mock us!?!"

"Oh, no, no! That's a cast iron, steel fence!"

"Very well. Then what is it that holds you back from standing with us? With the trees? Can't you see that at the current rate of deforestation and strip-mining the Earth will be left a barren parking lot within half a century?"

Arthur's attempt at humor—suggesting that maybe at least he'd finally be able to find a parking spot—did not go over well. He explained that he didn't remember much discussion of deforestation or strip-mining in the article.

"So there was greater emphasis on the profit-driven, corporate mentality's blind effort to ruin tomorrow's world for today's bottom line?"

"No, as I recall, most of the article was taken up with detailed descriptions of your unnatural, ungodly lifestyles. Is it true that you would push a fern out of the way of an on-rushing train before you'd save a newborn baby?"

Arthur: An Actuarial Odyssey

"What? Now listen up. I don't know what kind of anti-tree propaganda you've been handed, but this isn't about ferns versus babies. It's about the survival of the planet."

"Really? And isn't it true that you emotionally relate more easily with plant life than with your fellow human beings?"

"Look, forget all the lies they've crammed into your head. Just look around you."

"Okay."

"What do you see?"

"Six guys chained to trees."

"Beyond that. Take in the big picture. What do you see?"

"A big forest."

"Exactly. And what would you see if you were some bile-spewing, industrial profiteer?"

"Louisville Sluggers?"

"Precisely."

"Hey, I think I'm starting to get your meaning. These heartless, corporate scum are out to turn the simple, natural beauty of a tree in the forest into nothing but a piece of meat—to be bartered or sold."

"Something like that. So, you're with us?"

"Sure! Just one thing?"

Arthur: An Actuarial Odyssey

"What's that?"

"What are ya' doin'?"

"We've chained ourselves to these trees to put our bodies between the forest and the churning teeth of the corporate world's rapacious instruments of plunder."

"You mean chain saws?"

"If you prefer."

"And what's the plan when they get here with their instruments of plunder?"

"We will not yield!" The six raised their fists in the air.

"What exactly is the other option?"

"To place ourselves between the chain saw's blade and the tree! Are you with us, my friend?"

"Let's break this down. A guy gets here with a chain saw to cut down this tree."

"Right."

"He finds you chained to the tree and refusing to leave."

"Right."

"At which point, you defiantly challenge him to cut the tree down with you still attached."

"Right."

"And so what if he does?"

Arthur: An Actuarial Odyssey

"Then we shall have proven that the price of lumber is greater than the sanctity of life itself."

"Maybe I'm not getting something."

"There's nothing to get. We are out to stop the forest's destruction at all cost. As mere individuals we are expendable."

Arthur was torn. He thought their aim—saving the world of natural beauty from the clutches of greed and avarice—was a worthy cause. He sat on a rock to consider the matter. Here were these simple folk, dedicated and ready to face all odds. Their chanting started up again.

"So what do you say!?! Won't you join in a humble act of civil disobedience to save the forest?"

Arthur thought some more. It then struck him why he had come out to this desolate woodland in the first place. It was because he was sick and tired of taking the easy way out—living a life without purpose, without meaning. He'd come to re-dedicate his life to causes and questions greater than himself. He was here in search of answers. Answers to big questions. Consequently, Arthur explained he could not join in their selfless act of civil disobedience for he was far too busy in his cabin by the pond steeped in meaningful contemplation.

The environmental activists could not take no for an answer.

"Friend, let me tell you a story."

Arthur: An Actuarial Odyssey

"All right."

"It's about a simpler time, when many lived simpler lives."

"You mean the 70's?"

"Even before that."

"Go on."

"Well, there was this woman. She was not a young woman. She was a kindly older woman. She could have been anybody's grandmother."

"She could've been the grandmother of either Hitler or Gandhi?"

"Well, no—I mean anybody… Just any common person, regardless of fame."

"How could she have been both the grandmother of a common Chinese

person *and* a common Scandinavian person?"

The environmental activist began to turn a dark red and appeared quite angry. He conceded that the intended audience for his story was a lily-white, suburban, middle-class, stuck-in-the-50's romantic, but that it had a universal message that could be easily adapted to all cultural contexts. Not wanting to upset him further, Arthur sat back and listened.

"As I was saying, there was this kindly old woman. And she did not live too far from here in fact. She lived

Arthur: An Actuarial Odyssey

alone out in the woods for many years after her dear, beloved husband passed on."

Arthur began to weep. "Okay, okay, I understand."

"Hold on—that's not the point. There's more."

Arthur braced himself.

"One winter, on a bitterly cold and windy winter's night, as the little old lady sat alone in her cabin, the men in search of profits came trudging through the forest. But, alas, they had taken all the healthy trees and all that remained were trees that were either too sick or too young. So you know what they did?"

Arthur edged forward on his rock. "What?"

"When the little old lady invited them in for tea and biscuits—"

A chill ran up his spine, as the imagery struck a chord with Arthur's lily-white, suburban, middle-class, stuck-in-the-50's, romantic sensibility.

"—the forest robbers noticed a stack of logs by the fireplace which, with her arthritic back, it had taken the frail little old lady many months to collect last Spring."

Arthur gasped.

"Not three days later the men returned. The little old lady sat warming herself by the fire, knitting a scarf and sipping her tea. The winter's cold, dry air had been more than she'd expected that year and only a few logs remained. And so she sat, as the men crept their way in.

Arthur: An Actuarial Odyssey

Spying the last of her logs by the fireplace, the men sprang up, snatched the remaining logs and tore off into the woods, happy with themselves, already thinking about the hefty sums they would reap from the logs once they were turned into jewelry boxes. Later that night, not more than half a mile from this very spot, the wintry cold overcame that little old lady and she, like so many others, perished at the blood-soaked hands of corporate greed and plunder."

Arthur sat inconsolable.

"So you see. This is the meaning of our struggle. Either you stand with us and dead grandmothers. Or you stand with them—the grandma killers!"

"Then there can be no doubt. I am on the side of justice, plant life, and grandmothers!"

"So you'll join us?"

"Certainly. Hand me a padlock!"

The others cheered, as Arthur chained himself to a tree and the chanting resumed.

Soon thereafter, the chanting broke off as the feint echo of chain saw motors filtered through the forest. Eying one another, the environmental activists' resolve was re-doubled and they took up their chants with a renewed, forceful vigor.

"Preserve our Woodlands! Preserve our Woodlands!"

Arthur: An Actuarial Odyssey

The buzzing engines from the advancing army of chain saws grew louder.

"No to Wall Street, Yes to Hiking Trails! No to Wall Street, Yes to Hiking Trails!"

The instruments of plunder were practically upon them!

"Hey Hey, Ho Ho, Wiping Out the Forestland Has Got To Go! Hey Hey, Ho Ho, Wiping Out the Forestland Has Got To Go!"

Suddenly, through the brush and thickets, the chain saw-toting, tobacco-chewing, anti-nature arm of corporate rape and plunder came into view. Arthur seethed. There was no holding him back.

"Halt, you grandmother killers!" Arthur bellowed. "Your despicable acts of greed and avarice on behalf of the heartless, corporate bottom-liners ends here!"

There were five men in all. They cut off their chain saws and strolled over to the defenders of timber. One of the five immediately went for his cell phone. The others sat and waited. Apparently he was calling some big-shot corporate official to get the okay to continue with their ravenous destruction of the forest even at the cost of wasting a few tree-huggers. Arthur pictured the soul-less profiteer sitting in some posh 110th floor office, looking out over the glass and concrete-choked skyline, barking out orders to "clear out that section of forestland" or "go

Arthur: An Actuarial Odyssey

ahead and starve Bambi" cause "sales" needs to re-stock the inventory.

The tree-killer put away his phone and explained to the others that they'd have to wait for a call back. Arthur and the environmental activists resumed their chanting.

"Tree-Killers! Tree-Killers! Dirty, Rotten Nature Destroyers!"

The leader of the anti-forest, corporate mercenaries approached the group chained to trees.

"Nice day," he tried.

"Yeah, nice day for putting an end to greedy scum of the Earth, like the WORMS who handle the CHAIN SAWS OF DEATH AND MAYHEM!!!" Arthur shot back.

"Well, cancel my subscription to *Popular Mechanics* and get me on the next jet plane back to the stone age— looks like we've got ourselves a gen-yu-wine nature boy."

"Well, I guess, yeah—something like that." Arthur was slightly confused but remained resolute. "The point is we value natural beauty above corporate profit."

"Is that right?"

"Yeah... you see a forest and you see jewelry boxes and... and designer canoes and, you know... other stuff made out of wood."

Arthur: An Actuarial Odyssey

"And what do you see when you see a jewelry box or other stuff made out of wood?"

"The mangled remains of a butchered corpse," Arthur answered.

"Well, the way I see it, I'll take a good cigar box over a walk in the woods any day. Whadda ya think of that!?!"

"Why you—" Arthur had to hold himself back. This though posed little difficulty since he was chained to a 200-foot pine tree. The other environmental activists tried to calm him, explaining that the corporate mercenary was trained in techniques to incite environmental activists, coaxing them to unchain themselves and chase after them. This was exactly what they wanted so they could get on with their destructive ways. Arthur smirked and stared coldly into the gritty smile of the conniving mercenary.

"You're gonna have to do better than that—you endangered wildlife killer!"

As the two stared each other down, the clippity-clop of distant hoof beats was heard. It was the dreaded Sheriff Pinkerton, along with his deputies, to enforce a little justice. The six heavily armed, ideologically-duped thugs dismounted and moseyed over to the simmering stand-off. Arthur's tranquil oasis from the ugliness of the modern human condition was quickly spiraling into a tawdry scene of degenerative, social decay.

Arthur pulled the padlock snug to his chest and beckoned anyone who dared to smite him on the spot.

Arthur: An Actuarial Odyssey

This momentarily froze the army of corporate mercenaries, who—not wanting to seem ignorant—briefly huddled to weigh their options and to determine whether smiting, per se, was among them. After brief deliberation, the mercenaries decided to cut the environmental activists free from the chains and get on with their work.

As they approached Arthur's tree he let out a wild, primordial cry followed by a 45-second wolf howl and began belting out verses from "Ain't Gonna Let Nobody Turn Me Around." In his hyper-excited state, however, he mistakenly combined the words of "Ain't Gonna Let Nobody Turn Me Around" with the prior melody from "Fame." It was a horrible, sickening spectacle. The men ripped Arthur free of the tree, while still struggling to find his range. The armed mercenaries tossed Arthur and the environmental activists aside like toothpicks. Arthur fell against some rocks, scraping his ankle and tearing his shirt.

So these are the scars that battle brings, Arthur mused to himself. Regaining his composure, he readied himself to charge the corporate world's private army once more. Again they knocked him back upon the rocks.

"You mere stooges of capitalism!" Arthur cursed.

One of the environmental activists motioned the others to gather for a quick strategy session. They decided to once more put their bodies between the corporate world's instruments of plunder and the virgin forest's children.

Arthur: An Actuarial Odyssey

Rushing forward, they caught the mercenaries off guard and took up positions by the trees.

"He who pierces bark so doth he pierce flesh and bone!" cried Arthur.

The others once more took up the chant. The mercenaries had had enough. They moved in, rounded up Arthur and the environmental activists, and deposited them in the Bixby county jail. The conditions were barbaric.

Apparently Sheriff Pinkerton wanted to teach Bixby's social deviants a lesson. There was barely enough room for two of them to sit. The others squatted on the cold, concrete floor. The lighting was quite faint and the sink in their cell was one of those with separate faucets for cold and hot water so one could never quite control the temperature. The walls cried out for paint and the bars were a tetanus epidemic waiting to happen. But, thought Arthur, if this be the price of his convictions, so be it. Through it all, the six of them talked and laughed and giggled and sang. The Sheriff took his time with the paper work, a flickering black and white television humming in the background.

They shared the cell with two other intimidating brutes. One of them, leaning with a taciturn gaze against the cell door, claimed he'd shot a man "out West" and that he'd been brought in on some trumped up charge of driving with only one headlight.

"It's the system, Man!" Arthur philosophized.

Arthur: An Actuarial Odyssey

The inmate just stared straight ahead.

"No justice, no peace. Know what I'm sayin'?" Arthur exhorted.

His cell mate grasped the bars firmly with both hands without speaking.

"Well, keep the faith, eh cuz'?"

The inmate grunted affirmatively.

After some time, the other intimidating brute approached Arthur. This aroused Arthur's suspicions as he remembered reading about cases where—in the guise of a hardened criminal—prisons would put an undercover cop in a cell to collect information. Arthur was wise to this little charade from the get-go.

"So what're you boys in fer?" the suspicious brute asked.

Arthur had to think quickly. He'd always prided himself on his uncanny ability to think on his feet. "Let's just say," Arthur replied, "for doing bad things."

"Yeah. What kind of *bad* things?"

This guy was good, thought Arthur. "You see, it's like this. We're what they call a case of mystical identity."

"You mean *mistaken* identity?"

"Err, yeah, that's right—*mistaken* identity. We don't know who we are."

"I don't get it."

Arthur: An Actuarial Odyssey

"Well, you see it's like this"—the gymnastic workings of Arthur's quick mind was a sight to behold—"it's kind of a rare thing but occasionally there are these cases of group psychosis. Usually it's a single person who experiences temporary memory loss. But in our case—we all forgot who we were at the same time. As I say, it's a case of mistaken identity. We thought we were criminals so we came and turned ourselves in. But now we have remembered that we are businessmen from Denver."

The suspicious inmate didn't seem to be buying it. "So what kind of business?"

"Mail-order."

"And whadda ya sell?"

"Beach balls."

"And?"

"That's it. Just beach balls."

"You just sell mail-order beach balls?"

Suddenly Arthur felt he was sailing in unchartered waters. "Well, ya gotta understand, the market's just opening up. I mean we've got all kinds of different styles of beach balls designed for different demographic markets."

"I see. And what, for example, would you recommend for me?"

Arthur: An Actuarial Odyssey

Arthur knew he was being tested. "Well, let's see you're what 30-35, white male, 6 foot, about 200 pounds. Do you smoke?"

"Pack a day."

"Drink?"

"Excessively."

"Would you call yourself an extrovert or an introvert?"

"A what? Listen, I just wanna know what kind'a beach ball to get."

"Well, without completing our 'Me, Myself, and I Personality Verification Form' I can only give you a preliminary assessment, which would be to go with our model 11-c which is really a transitional beach ball between beach balls 10-f and 12-d. This is a beach ball which—while best highlighting the features of your personal essence—at the same time allows for room to grow and prepares you for your next beach ball which I imagine you will be ready for quite soon."

"How do I know you're not just making this stuff up?"

Arthur decided to go for a little reverse psychology. "And how do *I* know *you're* not just making up the fact that you think I'm making this up?"

"I'm not sure I could actually prove that I doubted you. I guess I'll just have to take my word for it."

"Exactly."

Arthur: An Actuarial Odyssey

"Hold on. I'm still confused."

"Correction. You *claim* that you're still confused. Just as I *claim* that I am a mail-order beach ball salesmen."

"Good point."

"Just trying to be consistent."

"So what're ya doin' way up here in Bixby? No beaches around here."

Arthur had to think quick. "We've been experimenting with a new forest beach ball—for the outdoorsman who loves the beach but can't get away."

"Sounds nuts."

"As I say it's still in the early, developmental stages. We've just begun the preliminary market research. Lumberjacks, for example, generally show no signs of a negative predisposition to the concept of a forest beach ball and upon prompting have been known to inflate and toss about said beach balls with one another during breaks."

The two were interrupted by the return of Sheriff Pinkerton. Apparently their bail had been taken care of by a sympathetic logging company from down state in competition with the company clearing the area near Arthur's cabin. Finally, thought Arthur, the savage world of cut-throat capitalist competition was paying off for the little guy. Following a highly emotional group hug and collective good-byes, Arthur returned to his cabin.

Arthur: An Actuarial Odyssey

Upon arriving, however, Arthur was horrified by what he found. His idyllic land of purity and innocence had been forever ripped from its foundation. First chain saws and then bulldozers had cleared a large swath through the forest near his cabin. An immense, towering billboard had been propped up in the middle of the clearing. It bore a message whose words could not have been more harrowing.

Site of Future Wal-Mart.

Making Your World a Little Less Commodity-Free.

Arthur collapsed. He knew he would have to leave this land and continue his search elsewhere. He tried to sleep that night but could only toss and turn as the glow from the flashing, neon Wal-Mart sign gave his cabin a distinct disco motif. He eventually drifted off to sleep with the haunting message—"Future Wal-Mart"—projected onto the wall just over his bed in bright blinking block letters.

Arthur: An Actuarial Odyssey

Chapter Eleven

The next day, Arthur collected his belongings and prepared for his painful re-immersion into society—a world from which he thought he had escaped only to be hunted down and re-baptized by the boundless reach of modern civilization's marauding, commercial agents. Morose and sullen, Arthur retreated from the virgin woodland. After nearly six months of desolate isolation, Arthur now wondered if his search for ultimate meaning and purpose was truly best pursued out in the untamed backlands anyway. Perhaps, he thought, a resumption of human contact would stir his senses and focus his thoughts more keenly.

With some fallen logs and a few tools abandoned by the tree-killers, Arthur was able to fashion a simple raft. He carried it to a nearby river and prepared to drift downstream and resume his search in some quiet, nondescript town. Quite tired, Arthur soon fell off to sleep. He awoke a few hours later to find that a strong current had pushed him out to sea. In a panic, Arthur

Arthur: An Actuarial Odyssey

began paddling for the nearest continent. With no land visible along the horizon, Arthur's crude raft was at the mercy of the frightful, ocean waters. After nearly two hours adrift and floundering on the open sea, Arthur came upon his salvation. Far off in the distance he spotted a ship easing across the waters. The ship's crew caught sight of Arthur's flailing arms and steered the massive vessel in his direction. Arthur soon found himself among the spirited crew of a Japanese whaling ship.

He was downing a bottle of sake with the others, as the ship's captain made his way over. The captain labored to light a thick, black pipe as he hustled across the deck barking out commands to his men. The captain was a short, heavy set man. He had steely, deep-set eyes with which he cast a menacing, devouring stare. Marking his approach was a slight limp to his swagger, the result of a crudely sculptured, wooden peg leg protruding from the captain's pant sleeve.

From a distance, through the rising puffs of smoke, Arthur could swear he recognized the captain—that he'd seen him somewhere before. His hair seemed shorter, his manner more coarse, and his Japanese completely unrecognizable, but there was something familiar about this Japanese, whaling ship taskmaster—this Captain Ahabu.

The two sat and briefly spoke through an interpreter. The captain explained that they were more than two weeks from their next port of call. There'd be no thought of heading in early, so Arthur was just going to have to

Arthur: An Actuarial Odyssey

wait it out. The captain was concise and business-like. Crew members explained that Captain Ahabu was under considerable strain these days and not to mind him. They said lately he was acting like a man obsessed. At any rate, it was best to just be patient and try not to cross him. Deciding to make the best of things and not wanting to antagonize the moody captain, Arthur volunteered to help out the crew however he could.

Arthur's first day of whale fishing did not begin well. He stood searching the waters off the portside for hours with the rest of crew, dangling his bait in the water. Then, after an insufferable, five-hour wait, finally, a whale was spotted. But just as their target came into view, a fatigued Arthur broke his long silence, shouting across the deck, "Hey, Shimamura, anymore of those rice balls left!?!" The whale took off like a shot. Captain Ahabu, who'd been spying Arthur from his cabin, slammed his door in disgust. Another four hours passed before the next opportunity.

Again, Arthur's inexperience showed. The look-out sent word of a whale sighting from the crow's nest on high. Captain Ahabu rushed on deck. Arthur and the others grabbed harpoons and leaned out over the water. All stood at the ready, waiting the order to throw. At last the whale came into view. It was right under Arthur's position. The shout went up. Arthur steadied himself and released his harpoon. Its weight was a bit more than anticipated, however, and he lost his balance in mid-toss. The others were forced to hold back their weapons as

Arthur: An Actuarial Odyssey

Arthur was left twisting over the side of the ship at the end of his safety line only a few feet above the water, stabbing madly at the sea with his harpoon.

Captain Ahabu ordered Arthur confined to his cabin for all future whale hunts. Arthur began to protest but then thought better of it. It would only be for two weeks and he really wasn't that excited about participating in the torturous murder of large, helpless mammals. He spent most of his time trying to avoid Captain Ahabu in a sea-tossed game of cat-and-mouse. Then one day, speaking to a crew member who'd studied English in the Swiss Alps, while living with Canadian exchange students, Arthur came to learn much more about this enigmatic Captain Ahabu.

"So tell me Keiji, what's the story behind his peg leg?"

Keiji seemed uneasy.

"Well, it's really best not to think of this matter, eh."

Arthur's curiosity was riled.

"Come on, how bad can it be?"

"Ok. But you didn't hear it from me."

"Sure, sure."

"Captain Ahabu doesn't talk much aboot it, eh. No one ever dares to mention anything aboot it in his presence."

Arthur: An Actuarial Odyssey

A stiff breeze crossed the ship's bow and the salty air filled the men's nostrils.

"Go on."

"Well, about 10 years ago, Captain Ahabu was the captain of a much smaller boat, eh. He and a crew of six were out whaling. It was a clear afternoon much like today—when he saw it."

The pounding waves splashed the men's feet.

"It?"

"It's tough to explain. You see, they'd been trailing a small school of whales for a couple of days. On the third day they decided to make their move."

The rolling sea softly rocked the ship beneath the two men's feet.

"And?"

"As I say, it's hard to say exactly, eh. They say the story is part truth, part lore. The crew and the captain though—they swear by it."

"So what happened?"

Keiji gnashed his teeth, leaned out over the rail, and stared hard into the blue horizon.

"They were just aboot to go for the kill, when a pair of speed boats appeared from out of nowhere full of crazed, environmental activists, eh."

Arthur's face lost all expression.

Arthur: An Actuarial Odyssey

"Captain Ahabu had faced down their kind before. That wasn't the problem."

"What was it then?"

"Off in the distance there was a large cruise ship—evidently filming a tv show or something. This is where details become hazy. Anyway, the environmental activists took off and commandeered the cruise ship in the distance, eh. And then... then they did the unthinkable."

"You mean..."

"That's right. They rammed Captain Ahabu's vessel with the Love Boat."

"Oh... My... God!"

"Captain Ahabu's ship was destroyed. In the melee he lost two crew members to the sea and his leg to a hungry shark. If it hadn't been for Gopher's quick action they say he may not have made it through alive."

"I can't believe it."

"The surviving crew members tried to make Captain Ahabu listen to reason. But he never could get the images of that day out of his mind, eh. They say that to this day he is obsessed with sailing the seas in desperate search of his mortal enemy—the Love Boat."

"But surely he realizes—"

"In his room, he still keeps a dart board with Captain Stubing's photo. On many a cold and wintry night he's been found just standing all alone on the upper deck,

Arthur: An Actuarial Odyssey

staring out into the sea mumbling to himself aboot one day finding that cursed Love Boat that sank his ship and took his leg. They say he will not rest until he settles the score."

As they spoke, the distinct thump of Captain Ahabu's limp could be heard approaching. The conversation turned to baseball, as the captain made his way past the two without a word. His familiar, gritty, determined stare tore through them like a laser. Arthur excused himself and returned to his cabin. He was convinced that Captain Ahabu was completely mad. He resolved to simply try to avoid him and wait it out until the next port of call.

Later that evening, however, Arthur was in his cabin dressing for the shuffle board tournament when it suddenly struck him where he had seen Captain Ahabu before. The captain was featured in the "Hall of Shame" section of a magazine that the environmental activists had shown him in jail. He was wanted in 18 countries for unspeakable crimes against the sea. Now, here was Arthur trapped aboard the heinous criminal's vessel. Insane or not, Arthur knew he had to stop this vile creature. He would need to somehow sneak into the control room and send out an emergency message to alert any environmental activists in the immediate area.

Arthur proceeded to the shuffle board tournament as though nothing were awry. Arriving late, Arthur hastily checked the line-ups and made his way over to his shuffle board match. A cold rush iced through his veins as he discovered that he and Keiji were to take on Hisashi and

Arthur: An Actuarial Odyssey

Captain Ahabu! Arthur took his position on the cold, clay surface beside Captain Ahabu who stood with stoic determination. Captain Ahabu got the match started, sending a puck swiftly along the playing surface to rest in zone three. Arthur steadied himself, beads of sweat coating his brow, and fired his puck after the captain's. He sent the captain's puck crashing off the board for a perfect placement of his own puck. Captain Ahabu breathed deeply with a simmering hate. Arthur waited nervously.

Now it was Arthur's turn to place the first puck. He was able to sit his right between zones one and two. Captain Ahabu's entire body shook with rage. He lined himself up to destroy Arthur's puck. In his fretful state, however, he launched his puck with tremendous force and it sailed wide right, smashing hard off the back of the playing surface by Hisashi's feet. Captain Ahabu sat down incensed. He could not even glance in Arthur's direction. Arthur stood a short distance away clutching his shuffle board cue as the others took their turns.

Captain Ahabu stood to again, all the more determined to dispatch with Arthur's puck. His steely eyes narrowed on their target. He grasped his cue tightly. All he saw was Arthur's face on that puck 30 feet away. He let out a high-pitched yelp and gave his puck a mighty push. Again he missed wide right. Captain Ahabu stood motionless, as Arthur prepared to put his next puck in play. Arthur's stroke was again spot on. A sickening, twisted sneer came over Captain Ahabu's face. He lit his pipe and sat now with his back to Arthur.

By this point, others had paused their matches to watch Arthur and Captain Ahabu contest. All stood silently. Arthur stepped into his box when again it was his turn. However, just as he released his puck across the playing surface, Arthur felt a sharp tug on his left heel. Captain Ahabu had snared Arthur's left foot with his shuffle board cue, disrupting him as he released his puck. Arthur fell forward and his puck bounded far off to one side. No one spoke a word. Captain Ahabu rose to take his turn. He placed his puck masterfully in zone three, as onlookers offered obsequious cheer. Arthur bristled. The two sat boiling with rage and the tension mounted. Keiji and Hisashi nervously took their turns and quickly sat.

Arthur grabbed his shuffle board cue, lined up his shot and ripped into Captain Ahabu's puck, replacing it in the zone three. Captain Ahabu snorted loudly, his face now beet red, and he sent his puck sailing after Arthur's. The crashing thud turned the heads of shuffle board players several matches away. Both pucks careened off the playing surface. Arthur thought he heard the captain mutter something about a "Captain Stubing wannabe." But the two took their seats without incident.

Captain Ahabu moved to the rail along the deck as Keiji and Hisashi took their turns. The match continued in this manner for hours. The pressure palpable. With each player's advance the other would be left seething. Finally, the match was nearing a close. As their final turns came, the two found themselves in a dead heat. Arthur crossed the shuffle board surface to line up his approach. His concentration was fixed on zone three, 30 feet away. He bent his knees, cocked his shoulders back, stepped into his thrust, and released the puck. It was a stunning placement. The entire match now came down to Captain Ahabu's final play.

Captain Ahabu settled into position, nestling his puck with his cue. For the first time, he glanced over at Arthur, offering a sneering, confident look of contempt. Arthur glared back. Captain Ahabu felt the shuffle board cue in his hand, centered his puck, and squared to line up his shot. He eyed Arthur's perfectly placed puck, looked down at his own, set himself, and gave his puck a forceful lunge along the playing surface. As the puck raced along the board, it was as if time itself had slowed to watch. Arthur stood, fixed on the board and nervously dropping his shuffle board cue. Captain Ahabu stood, gawking after his puck and gesticulating wildly with his hands. Others stretched their necks spellbound. Captain Ahabu's puck careened off Arthur's with a heart-sinking thud. Both pucks came to rest just off the playing surface. The match was a draw.

Captain Ahabu stood crestfallen. As Arthur gathered his things, Captain Ahabu circled the shuffle board surface and jostled past Arthur to quickly depart. On passing Arthur, Captain Ahabu mouthed something under his breath. Keiji later explained that the captain had said, "So, round one ends even. We shall see about our next

Arthur: An Actuarial Odyssey

clash." Arthur hustled back to his cabin. He knew he hadn't much time.

Arthur: An Actuarial Odyssey

Chapter Twelve

Arthur lay awake that night, his mind racing with volcanic speed, plotting how he might break into the control room and get a message out over the ship's radio. He beamed with boyish pride at having had the foresight years ago to take that Navy Seals correspondence course in preparation for moments just like this. He was kicking himself, however, for not having taken the extra-credit unit on "How to Sneak Into the Control Room of a Japanese Whaling Ship." There was no PO box to write for tutorial assistance or 800 number to call for helpful hints now. Not out here in the real world of daring-do. By daybreak, Arthur had the outline of his ingenious plan.

Already making use of the Navy Seals top secret memorization technique, he retained the precise lay-out of the entire ship in his mind's eye. Arthur assigned each room a letter. The first room was "A." The second was "B." The third was "R." This was where the top secret element came in. If a Navy Seal was captured it was his

Arthur: An Actuarial Odyssey

sworn duty never to reveal the clandestine Navy Seal alphabet. The correspondence school had trained Arthur to withstand unspeakable acts of torture without revealing that alphabet. He had been through numerous "torture drills" designed—the school assured—to "break even the most seasoned professional."

The school was renowned for two drills in particular. International spy agencies from around the world sent their top agents to the school for training in these make-or-break exercises. First, Arthur was forced to endure the "Ostracized Liberal Torture Test." Trainees were sent a special Undercover Liberal Training Kit. Among its items was a bumper sticker which read: "Hoping for the day when the schools will have all the money that they need and the Army will have to hold bake sales for a new bomber." They were instructed to place it on a bright red convertible VW Bug and drive past the nearest military installation with the top down, wearing bell bottoms, beads, a vintage '70's "hippie" wig, multi-colored elevator shoes and a "love and peace" head band—all provided in the kit.

Arthur's test was particularly grueling. Always wanting to go that extra mile, Arthur defiantly threw flowers at military personnel as he passed along the route. Arthur held up well. The intimidating stares, cruel taunting, suggestive gestures, and hurtful words would've broken a lesser person. But Arthur just answered with a flower and a smile. He was surviving the torture test splendidly. Then, suddenly, events took a perilous turn.

Arthur: An Actuarial Odyssey

Just after tossing a bright rose to a particularly enraged, 350-pound sergeant, Arthur's convertible suffered a flat. Arthur hastily got out to change the tire, tripping over his bell bottoms and catching the tire iron in his love beads. A mob of crew cuts quickly gathered. Arthur worked fast. The throng was closing in, their jeers becoming more and more personal in nature. Arthur put the spare in place and lowered the jack. The crowd was right up on him. He tightened the nuts under a hail of venomous, pro-Army, anti-cupcake remarks. Things looked as if they might turn ugly just as Arthur jumped back into the convertible, losing an elevator shoe on the door handle. He sped off tossing out flowers, as the mob stood shouting obscenities and waving his elevator shoe in frustration.

The Navy Seals correspondence course's second torture test was even more arduous. Trainees were sent to Kid Rock concerts wearing nothing but sandals, shorts, a Mr. Rogers T-shirt, and a propeller beanie. The entire time there they were instructed to loudly hum the melody of the Village People's "YMCA." As if this weren't conspicuous enough, between sets, trainees were instructed to shout out suggestions that the band add more African-American women and openly gay members. At the same time, they were instructed to circulate a petition among Kid Rock enthusiasts to pass the ERA and fight homophobia.

Arthur at first mixed fairly easily into the right wing, reactionary Hitler youth, their shaven heads, protruding

Arthur: An Actuarial Odyssey

bellies, and adoring Kid Rock attire prominently displayed. While Mr. Rogers drew stares, Arthur's rendition of "Macho, Macho Man" seemed to keep people at bay. The petition drive, however, was not going well. He'd only been able to gather a handful of stoned concert-goers' illegible signatures. Furthermore, trouble was brewing. A couple of alienated, ideologically adrift, young, white males overheard Arthur's imploring a young woman to "break the chains of patriarchal subjugation and castrate the oppressor with a defiant commitment to anti-misogynist, feminist struggle!" Fortunately for Arthur, just as the two prepared to confront him, someone accidentally elbowed them from behind, prompting an all-out, chair-swinging, retaliatory assault. Arthur took care to move on.

On other occasions Arthur was able to avert close calls with drunken white supremacists by cleverly asking, "Hey, is that guy over there giving you the finger?" Things took a turn for the worse, however, when between sets Arthur decided to ad lib and call out for a Tracy Chapman medley. The entire stadium fell into a stunned and disoriented silence. They sensed an interloper. Kid Rock stepped to the edge of the stage to get a look at the blasphemer. All that could be heard was Arthur's feint humming. As all eyes fastened on Arthur. He knew it was time for his patented, correspondence school Navy Seals escape. He shouted out, "Oh sorry, I meant Barry Manilow" and bolted for the exit with an entire Kid Rock

Arthur: An Actuarial Odyssey

concert crowd chasing after him. That was one Navy Seals training drill that Arthur barely got out of alive.

Arthur's plans for sending out an emergency message from the control room, meanwhile, were proceeding on schedule. With each room of the whaling ship assigned a letter and its detailed interior lay-out committed to memory, Arthur set out to put Lesson Two of his Navy Seal correspondence school training to work. He had to learn the daily schedules of key crew members. Arthur casually strolled on deck, not wanting to arouse any suspicions. Standing by the rail, at a deceptively oblique angle he'd been specially trained to utilize, Arthur spied the captain and his navigator going over maps in the control room. The time was 7:05—that's ante meridiem.

Arthur made a mental note and quite unsuspiciously moseyed further along the deck. At precisely 7:28 he observed the lookout sentry in the crow's nest climbing down from his perch to be relieved. For a trained mind such as Arthur's this became a mental note without even thinking to make it a mental note. By 8:22 all but three members of the crew were eating breakfast. The Captain ate alone in his cabin. Needing a clever ruse to exit during breakfast, sheer inspiration led Arthur to spill steaming, hot coffee on his lap. The Navy Seals correspondence school training taught all its students to withstand the placement of boiling, hot liquids upon their skin by screaming hysterically and frantically rushing from rooms. This was just the ploy Arthur needed to check the

Arthur: An Actuarial Odyssey

whereabouts of the other three crew members at this critical hour.

One sat in the crow's nest. One casually mopped along the starboard side of the ship's stern. The other sat quietly in the control room on the ship's bow. Again, Arthur committed all this to an air-tight memory and returned to breakfast. He otherwise passed the day in ordinary fashion, calling upon his special undercover training for everyday inconspicuousness to make both his motives and his movements all but invisible to the untrained eye. Arthur had done particularly well on the "undercover" section of the correspondence training.

He'd earned the correspondence school's top marks on the "undercover" exam. The stealth exam called for students to successfully conceal the fact that they were taking a Navy Seals training course from one's closest friends and family members. The school then contacted a random friend or family member of the student to test if their cover had been blown. When they called Arthur's closest friends and family members they not only knew nothing about the Navy Seals training course, most could not even say what he'd been up to since leaving junior high.

So Arthur spent the day stealthily going about his business by stealthily going about his business. Not wanting to draw attention to his secret, environmental activist agenda, Arthur took as many opportunities as he had to share with fellow crew members his great love for the maiming and killing of desperate, flailing beasts. Yes,

Arthur: An Actuarial Odyssey

Arthur explained, the fresh, hot scent of a bloodied corpse wafting through his port hole in the morning, that was what he truly needed to get himself out of bed each day.

Arthur even took time over lunch to tell a few others how, for him, the whale hunt was a total, almost mystical experience; the rush of adrenaline as the chase commenced; the cold, salty spray slapping cheek and jowl as one leaned out from the ship, harpoon at the ready; the heat rising from the carcass as his cold, steel blade cut and gutted the animal. No, nothing like an old fashioned mammal-on-mammal, whale hunt for a true lover of whale hunts like he definitely was, Arthur assured.

Arthur left the lunch room smiling smugly. He had carried out Lesson 3 of the Navy Seals correspondence course—"Throwing off Any Undue Suspicions"—in textbook fashion. To the crew he was just another impassioned whale hunting enthusiast. No one suspected that, in fact, they were witnesses to a professionally-trained Navy Seal in action as an undercover environmental activist. Faultlessly brilliant as he was, his cover was very nearly blown just moments later when he stood looking out over the stern laughing uproariously and screaming out into the sea, "Hah! Such fools! They'll never catch on! Not to a genius like me!" As he spoke, the captain passed along the deck and overheard the otherwise coy Arthur's boastful rantings. His English was not perfect but what he understood he did not like.

Speaking through Keiji, he demanded that Arthur explain exactly what he meant. Arthur froze. He had to

Arthur: An Actuarial Odyssey

quickly refer back to his Navy Seal training for guidance. The answer came to him instantly. He told the captain that he'd been coaxing the whales to appear by first provoking them with incendiary remarks about them and their kind. Still unsettled by his mishaps earlier in the week, Arthur assured the captain that he merely hoped to make amends by filling the seas with personally-affronted whales for the slaughter. Captain Ahabu bought it and told Arthur to carry on. So Arthur returned to the rail, shouting filthy slurs at the defenseless sea life swimming or floating nearby. After so close a call, Arthur returned to his cabin for the remainder of the day.

That night the final details of his plan were put into place. In the morning, during the breakfast hour, Arthur would make his move. He confronted three obstacles. First, having already used the "spilling of boiling, hot liquids" technique he would need a new ruse for suddenly excusing himself from breakfast. Second, on his way to the control room he had to make it past the lookout's post, the mopping crew member, and the munching captain's cabin. Third, once past the lookout, the mopper, and the captain, Arthur would need to neutralize the lone crew member left in the control room during the breakfast hour.

For his hasty withdrawal from breakfast, Arthur would rely on the Navy Seal's fallback maneuver—the slightly more risky "Oh-My-God-These-Aren't-My-Pants" technique. This particular maneuver relied almost entirely on the element of surprise. If executed properly, the exiter will have actually left the room before others can assess the claim.

The next morning Arthur headed down to breakfast. His casual, nonchalant demeanor did not betray the scheme still hatching in his mind. He sat near the door— though not too near the door, perchance the coincidence of abruptly taking his leave and his having sat so near an exit might raise eyebrows. He chewed some bread, biding his time. Then at the precisely perfect moment, his Navy Seals training kicked in. He stood in a flash, creating an audible woosh and, quoting the manual verbatim, he screamed, "Oh my God, these aren't my pants!" Acting with supreme polish, he bolted from the room before the exclamation point had even left his mouth. Once outside, he double-checked to assure that no one had followed him out. With the coast clear, the operation shifted to phase B.

Concealed from view, standing beside a large canister, Arthur gingerly turned to spot the mopping crew member. Just as his scouting foretold, the mopper was a good distance away with no clear sight-line of the control room. He had effectively been removed from the equation by Arthur's uncanny execution of his Navy Seals' incognito training. Next was the look-out. Again, from his surveillance the prior day he knew that the look-out had just begun his shift in the crow's nest. Hence, his attention was directed out to sea, studying the water's surface for any whale activity. With respect to the look-out, Arthur merely had to maneuver carefully, making

Arthur: An Actuarial Odyssey

sure that his sly, cat-like moves did not draw the eagle eye's curiosity.

Lastly, to reach the control room Arthur would have to pass beneath Captain Ahabu's cabin window. Arthur knew the captain would be eating alone in his room and so he had merely to slither past the digesting ogre. As it happened, the captain played his radio quite loudly, making Arthur's professionally-trained slithering that much easier. Then, nearly past Captain Ahabu's cabin, in mid-slither, he felt a sharp tug on his pant leg. Arthur anxiously looked back. He had snagged himself on a distended bolt. He quickly freed himself and continued. In freeing himself, however, Arthur had inadvertently dropped a pack of condoms, a blue promotional pen from Sea World, and a Polaroid snap-shot of an identifying-scar on the back of his left shoulder. Oblivious to his momentary lapse, Arthur's faux pas could not have been more damning.

Arthur crawled onward to the control room. The deck's steel surface left Arthur's forearms bruised and bloodied. His clothes were soaked by the seas' relentless, pounding waves. But Arthur was a man possessed. Ahead, he saw the outline of the crew member standing by the map desk in the control room with his back to the door. Arthur slid his battered body across the ocean-tossed whaling ship's deck. The plan was proceeding like clock-work. He closed in on the control room, quietly pulled himself to the door's threshold and stood in the heavy, steel door's shadow. Arthur then pulled the

Arthur: An Actuarial Odyssey

bowling pin—which he had ingeniously told the others was a cigarette lighter—from his belt and prepared to subdue the crew member.

Arthur sprang upon him in a single motion. The hapless crew member had time only to plead with Arthur in his broken English, "But I no smoke!" It was over that quickly. However, the thud of the crew member hitting the control room floor was louder than Arthur anticipated. Loud enough, in fact, to catch the ear of Captain Ahabu, who stepped outside his cabin to investigate. Finding nothing, he was about to return inside when the odd collection of items at his feet caught the captain's keen eye.

Captain Ahabu may not have been some highfalutin phi beta kappa, but he knew how to put two and two together. When he spotted a pack of condoms, a pen from SeaWorld, and the Polaroid of a scar on the back of someone's left shoulder, Captain Ahabu sensed something was astir. Initially, it was only evident that somewhere on board there was an animal-loving, conspicuously-scarred, safe sex practitioner. Captain Ahabu further pondered the matter. Then, studying the pen more closely, he found the incriminating inscription: "To the whale lover in all of us—Love, Flipper." Upon further reflection, the captain recalled how he had earlier written it off as a mere quirk when he'd seen Arthur occasionally move among the crew members to say hello and remind one and all not to forget to go with latex when "doing the nasty." In disgust, the captain tossed the pen and condoms into the churning seas and set out to capture this vile creature infecting his vessel.

Meanwhile, Arthur dragged the unconscious crew member off to the side and immediately went to work. He grabbed the radio and began barking out commands.

"May day! May day! This is an emergency! Calling all environmental activists! Calling all environmental activists! The loathed and dreaded Captain Ahabu has set sail upon these very seas! Need help to halt his evil ways! Repeat, need help to halt—"

Suddenly, the menacing, peg-legged figure of Captain Ahabu filled the doorway.

Arthur was smooth. "Oh hey, Captain. Just checking the equipment."

Captain Ahabu reached out and tore off Arthur's shirt, revealing the identifying scar on the back of his left shoulder. Realizing that his cover had been blown, Arthur deftly switched strategies.

"Hah! Your evil ways are over Captain! May day! May day!"

Captain Ahabu ripped the radio controls from Arthur and wrestled him to the floor. He snared an iron rod near the control board and swung for Arthur's head. Arthur rolled to his left and dashed for the door. But Captain Ahabu tripped him with his peg leg and Arthur smashed headlong into a fire hydrant. Snatching the hydrant, Arthur sprayed Captain Ahabu, briefly disorienting him.

Arthur: An Actuarial Odyssey

The captain stood flailing wildly with the iron rod, as Arthur escaped by a side door and raced to the end of the bow, with the foam-covered, rod-wielding, peg-legged captain in clumsy pursuit.

Arthur ran himself into a corner. Breathing heavily, the two stared each other down. Arthur told captain Ahabu he would never get away with this. But threatening a mad man who'd cornered him at the end of a ship, swinging an iron rod out on the high seas did not seem Arthur's best move at this juncture. Now toying with him, captain Ahabu slowly pressed Arthur further into a corner. The dire limitations of studying hand-to-hand combat through a correspondence school were quickly becoming apparent to Arthur. Then, glancing out at the expansive seascape, and relying solely on his specially-trained Navy Seals instinct, Arthur spied a distant ship moving across the horizon.

His hands rubbed raw clenching the rail, Arthur held his ground bobbing and weaving to avoid the blow of Captain Ahabu's lethal, iron rod. The remote ship drew nearer. The menacing captain Ahabu swung still harder. Arthur eyed the closing ship. He looked back to captain Ahabu. Again putting his Navy Seals training to work—more precisely Lesson 11, "Escaping Ill-Fate Upon Japanese Whaling Boats and Elsewhere"—Arthur quickly surveyed the situation and came to an instantaneous, in-the-field, textbook Navy Seals assessment.

His message having successfully gotten out (that is, his mission complete), Arthur knew it was time to close this chapter of his life as an undercover, environmental activist. He dove into the icy waters and headed toward the other ship. This proved difficult at first, insofar as the Navy Seals correspondence course adamantly instructed its students to avoid swimming lessons at all cost.

The theory was that Navy Seals were celebrated as expert swimmers. Therefore, were Arthur to display such expertise this may divulge his secret training to others. Thus, putting his professional training to work, down to the final details, Arthur dog-paddled the half-mile or so to the waiting ship.

Arthur: An Actuarial Odyssey

Chapter Thirteen

Arthur reached the massive vessel weak and weary and grabbed hold of a life-line the ship's crew tossed down to him. Looking above, he was momentarily disoriented by a fierce, white light that drowned out the sky. Clearing his head and glancing up once more, he saw the happy, smiling faces of what turned out to be the deliriously perky deck attendants aboard a luxury cruise liner. Their larger-than-life smiles and immaculately clean teeth at first blinded Arthur. The crew members pulled his limp body toward the teeth and he boarded the cruise ship. After sharing his harrowing exploits, the sympathetic teeth led Arthur to an empty cabin to rest.

Arthur slept several hours, before leaving the cabin later that evening to look about. He found a brochure near the Delirious Pandemonium Lounge. He had apparently boarded The Happy Camper Cruise Line which was on its way to "10 glorious, fun-in-the-sun days and nights of unrepentant, carnal splendor." Still reeling from his

Arthur: An Actuarial Odyssey

frightening escape from a Japanese whaling ship, Arthur toasted his good fortune at the Jim Dandy Good Time Saloon. After his life-and-death struggles with Captain Ahabu, Arthur settled in to enjoy the velvet-gloved pampering of the hospitable army of teeth who had taken pity on him in his frail, sea-tossed condition.

Arthur looked over the agenda for the next few days, while sitting by the pool in his complementary silk speedos and ignoring the occasional admiring glance. His week was looking pretty full. He'd begin with the 1,004 Fingers Massage in the Inhibitionless Spa and Whirlpool. Then he'd top the evening off with a harmless bout of full-contact volleyball or perhaps a movie. Tonight was "Jingoistic Film Night"— with a double feature of *Red Dawn* and the reinterpretation of a classic, *Guess Who the Hell's Not Coming to Dinner*. Yes, thought Arthur, this would be a nice transition back from months of solitary woodland contemplation and his recent skirmish with Captain Ahabu.

Every few minutes a new set of teeth would pass by, asking Arthur if he needed anything. Each time, Arthur would explain that all he needed was to be turned into a bird, set free, and allowed to soar the skies above the earth's enslaving gravity. The teeth generally came back with a Sprite. Arthur wiped the condensation from the glass, adjusted the towel draped across his shoulders, and let the cool, bubbly liquid smack the back of his throat and trickle down his body. Reclining in an adjustable chair, his fingers felt the arm rest for the radio dial, as the

Arthur: An Actuarial Odyssey

deck chair's surround sound softly lifted him away on the mellow chords of a Barry White medley.

Dinner that evening would be served in the Culinary Hedonist's Dining Room, complete with a Guy Lombardo Fixin's Bar. Attendants sprayed the room with a light rose mist which still lingered in the air. An assortment of easy-listening favorites lent chewing a pleasant rhythmic splendor. Sets of teeth periodically moved among the tables to maintain a proper level of selfless servitude. As he swallowed, Arthur's attention turned to the other coddled Happy Camper Cruisers. It felt ever so like a wholesome reflection of small town, U.S.A.—the type of town where he himself had grown up.

Why, there by the door was the Reverend Jebediah and his family. And not far from them was a typical, middle-class family enjoying their meal—oh, that rascal little Bobby stole a chicken wing right off his sister's plate. There beneath a looming portrait of Lou Henry Hoover—the lovable former first lady and accomplished Chinese linguist—sat a small cluster of typical, small family farmers, so sturdy, brave, and true. They were the hearty bedrock of every small town. Up towards the front, wiping the roast beef's bloody juices from their fat, round jowls, sat the bankers who—ever faithful to the natural laws of predatory capitalism—had foreclosed on the land of many of those small, family farmers.

Restricted to a cramped cabin in an isolated area below deck near the engine room and now seated near the

Arthur: An Actuarial Odyssey

kitchen door, one could see the upwardly mobile Jones family. As one of the few middle class Black families, they were, naturally, feared and loathed as an existential threat to the inherited social privileges of the white citizenry and had been accordingly shunned and run out of town. And there, off in a back corner, sat a small group of out-of-wedlock, pregnant adolescent girls. The absentee fathers, whom everyone in town knew so well, sat drunk and happy near the bar, apparently still needing to sow a few more wild oats.

Such a truly small, small world, thought Arthur. Here aboard this luxury liner Arthur could find the same socioeconomic mix and venal bigotry that still made small town America that idyllic icon of an innocent, romanticized past. Lost in thought, gazing upon the Culinary Hedonist Dining Room's impressive rendering of that unique American cultural patchwork of denial, betrayal, and misery, Arthur suddenly noticed he would be late for the evening's festive film—"Red Dawn." Seated a bit too close to the NRA table, he was nearly trampled when the call went out that the film would begin in two minutes.

After the film, as the Happy Camper Cruise Line brochure explained, passengers were invited to "spend the romantic, moonlit, midnight hours shooting at the stars on the Good-Old-Boys Pistol Range." After a full day, however, Arthur passed on the "good times for all" at the firing range and headed to bed. As he put out the light to sleep, the soothing sounds of gentle waves kissing the

Arthur: An Actuarial Odyssey

ship's hull were piped into his cabin by an elaborate intercom system running stern to bow throughout the entire cruise liner.

Passengers were able to "adjust" the size of the waves with dials in their cabin. Thinking he had silenced the waves, Arthur had apparently only turned it to the lowest setting. He worked on the pipes in his bathroom for nearly an hour until he discovered that the sound of water dripping from a leaky faucet was coming from the speakers. This was no good. When re-set at the highest level, the system simulated tidal wave conditions, complete with warning sirens and emergency crews shouting evacuation plans every ten minutes through a megaphone.

Arthur readjusted things once more and settled for sleeping beside a babbling brook that evening. He could discuss matters in detail with a pair of teeth in the morning. This setting, however, proved the most disagreeable of all, as it seemed some jokester had rejiggered the "babbling brook" feature such that all one heard was the voice of the brook going on and on, talking endlessly about itself. Arthur eventually drifted off, after returning to the original "gentle waves" setting.

Arthur woke early the next morning for an invigorating jog and aerobics workout before a hearty breakfast. He traced the full perimeter of the Happy Camper Cruise Line deck numerous times. He'd never felt so alive, so free, so full of life. After his jog, Arthur joined a small crowd of spandex worshipers, bouncing up

Arthur: An Actuarial Odyssey

and down in front of another set of teeth to the pulsating rhythms of "She Works Hard for Money." Arthur eased his way into the gyrating mob, as he mouthed the words, "so you better treat her right."

The teeth, keeping with the demanding, can-do spirit of the aerobics workout, welcomed Arthur with a rousing, "Come on lardo, let's lift those knees. That's it, I wanna see this boat tilt your way. And a one, and a two…"

Arthur stretched the palms of his hands skyward, swaying to the musical beat while marching in place. Listening to the motivational teeth's words of encouragement Arthur had the strong sense that he had seen this particular set of teeth somewhere before. Momentarily lost in thought, he missed when the others graduated to a new routine. He continued reaching skyward as they moved their hands to their hips and began a step-out, step-in sashaying motion.

"Yo, are we at a high degree of difficulty for you there Mr. Chocolate-Eclair-Poster-Boy?"

That guttural voice, the subtle sarcasm it all seemed so familiar. Arthur caught up with the group and squinted hard for a better view of the teeth. In an instant things made sense. He couldn't believe his eyes. It was Felicia Philips! After all these years. Why, the last time he'd seen Felicia—it seemed so silly now—but it was just before their senior prom. After going steady for three years, he dumped her to go out with a gorgeous blond who had just transferred to their school. Felicia thus attended the prom

Arthur: An Actuarial Odyssey

all alone and forlorn, while Arthur and Bambi were voted the prom's cutest couple. Well, thought Arthur, surely bygones must be bygones. It was all so long ago. Arthur's momentary lapse again put him out of sync with the now bouncing aerobics class.

"What's the matter, tubby—no *Bambi* to help tell you your left foot from the right?"

Apparently, all was not forgotten. Arthur smiled playfully, thinking that her words had no doubt been meant in good humor. But just then, the bouncing teeth vanished. In their place appeared the worn and haggard face of a love-starved, middle-aged woman, whose desperate search for companionship had led to a torturous life of aerobics, cruise ships, and tequila shots. Arthur tried to ease his way to the back row.

"Alright everybody," shouted an enthusiastic, bouncing Felicia, "Let's all find a partner."

Everyone quickly paired up. Arthur, arriving late and alone, was left standing by himself.

"Well Romeo, looks like it's gonna be you and me," Felicia scoffed.

Arthur reluctantly crossed the deck and stood beside Felicia.

"Now I want everyone to take a good look at their partner. This will be your aerobics partner for the duration of the cruise. This will require a complete team effort. So it is very important that no one sleep late or

Arthur: An Actuarial Odyssey

miss a class—or you'll have no one but your partner to answer to. Now, I want everyone to go through these next exercises at you and your partner's own pace."

Felicia instructed each team to break down for sit-ups. One partner did the sit-ups while the other counted. Arthur's back hit the mat, as Felicia began to count after she restarted the tape deck and the aerobics class resumed, reclining and rising to the syncopated rhythms of the "Kojak" theme song. At first, Felicia kept a steady, regular count. But she soon picked up the pace. Arthur adjusted well at first. Before long, though, he could feel the mat burning into his lower back. Felicia's steady, regular cadence became a hate-filled, vengeful command. She experienced a complete metamorphosis. With each sit-up he caught a glimpse of Felicia's transformation—her bulging eyes and snarling lips. He was nearing complete exhaustion—his pulse racing, his brow soaked in sweat. At last, she called out for all pairs to switch off.

Arthur now knelt, holding Felicia's ankles, his energy evaporated. On the verge of physical collapse, he half-heartedly kept count of Felicia's progress. Her relentless demand for Arthur to, "Count faster! Faster!" echoed in his ear, drowning out the music. But Arthur could count no faster. His reprieve only came with the ringing of the breakfast bell. This signaled for everyone on board to halt all activities and make their way in rapid but orderly fashion to the Beaming with Sunshine Breakfast Room.

Arthur returned to the world of unadulterated rest and relaxation. He was confident that Felicia's mood would

Arthur: An Actuarial Odyssey

have time to mellow by the next morning. After a hearty Happy Camper Cruise Line breakfast Arthur briefly visited the Happy Camper Cruise Line Museum. The ship's entire history was recounted here. First set afloat in 1979, it was first christened The Large Vacationing Floating Object. With poor initial sales, The Large Vacationing Floating Object was soon countermanded at sea and set ablaze just off the coast of Aruba in a scheme to collect the insurance money.

Nearly two-thirds of the ship was destroyed and, though deaths and injuries were kept to a minimum, the ship's owners were forced to reimburse many of the disgruntled vacationers. Facing bankruptcy, the ship was sold, rebuilt, and re-named the Happy Camper Cruise Line in 1982. The initial years of operation were lean. But in 1985 a new management team was put to work to re-fashion the ship's image, following the widely-publicized fire and a slew of failed promotional packages that had followed the fire when the Happy Camper Cruise Line first set sail.

The optional, reduced-rate rowing package was immediately dropped. The Bring-Your-Own-Navigator special group rate was ended, as well. Other less-than-successful promotional ploys were re-worked. Food orders were re-doubled so that passengers caught returning to the buffet line for seconds no longer faced the inconvenience of being customarily stranded at the next available port. The slide shows of the captain's family vacations were completely replaced by actual,

Arthur: An Actuarial Odyssey

day-long dockings at various ports. Over the years, the ships full complement of amenities had gradually expanded to make this "the premiere ocean-going good-time the world over." It was clear that the Happy Camper Cruise Line had come a long way since its troubled beginnings.

Arthur left the Happy Camper Cruise Line Museum with a strong sense of its proud history. His spirit renewed, he went for a brief, brisk walk along the deck, awash in the memories of its legendary past. He stopped along the ship's bow to taste the cool, ocean breeze. The sun glistened off the breaking water's surface. A pair of lovers sat nearby. The two were quarreling, as all young couples surely do from time to time. The quaintness of a lover's spat against the backdrop of the ocean's horizon brought to mind long-past, romantic memories for Arthur—a time of innocence and blissful wonder.

The fair maiden reproached her young suitor, "I can't believe you slept with that bitch!"

"But babe, I swear it didn't mean nuthin'," her lover softly intoned. "The whole time I... I felt so dirty."

Arthur moved along, lifted by the refreshingly honest passions of young lovers. He lingered awhile in the We Love Quarters Game Room where he could choose from an assortment of games designed to "simulate the vengeful killing of an assortment of communists, aliens, and Arabs, or the rescuing of scantily-clad babes from the clutches of un-American, un-pale goons, while appealing

Arthur: An Actuarial Odyssey

to the little kid in all of us," An hour or so of plump, 40-something men strutting about with their pockets jingling full of quarters and screaming "Die you lousy Gook!" into blinking video screens proved enough for Arthur, who returned to his cabin before lunch.

He spent the afternoon resting up for his evening's big event, re-reading *Little Women* and crying like a baby every time he came to the final twenty pages which he kept forgetting had been ripped out. He drew only blank stares when asking other passengers if he could borrow their copy for a night. All this was soon forgotten in the excitement of the evening's other planned merriment. Arthur's pent-up anticipation quickly waned, however, when the evening's carnival of fun was marred by tragedy.

Apparently no one had thought through all of the potential difficulties for a full-scale production of the Ice Capades at sea. A team of teeth had worked the entire afternoon icing down a large section of the deck. While the show started out spectacularly enough, it was only five minutes into the second set before the ship's gentle motion sent six or seven skaters skidding uncontrollably over the starboard side. A pair of rescue teams then skillfully plucked each of them from the icy waters. The crowds impassioned cry for the ensemble to "give it one more try" was not enough for them to overcome their hypothermia and the Ice Capades show had to be canceled. Arthur tried working the crowd some more for a copy of *Little Women* before eventually turning in.

Arthur: An Actuarial Odyssey

He awoke the next day and set out on his jog, having forgotten the silliness of the previous day's aerobics workout. His morning jog went pleasantly. Everyone he passed that morning seemed especially chipper. Utter gaiety and bliss were etched across their happy faces. It shown in that extra-friendly greeting, that extra-bouncy bounce in their step. Arthur proceeded on to his aerobics class, assured that the morning horizon's new sun brought with it a new day, a new attitude, and a new Felicia.

Again among the last to arrive, Arthur squeezed his twisting, pulsating, spandex-encased body into the mix—this time eliciting no comment from Felicia. Finding it far easier to focus than the day before, Arthur melted into the aerobic action with a natural, effortless ease. While lifting his knees high into the air and twisting his torso to the left, then to the right, he began to notice something slightly odd about that day's class. It seemed—looking to and fro—that he did not see very many of the obscenely obese revelers from yesterday. He gathered that, for whatever reason, they had thought to drop out. So this day, though he did not consider himself especially unshapely, Arthur did note that he was one of the less physically fit members of the class.

The workout continued much as the prior morning, but with a tamer, more subdued Felicia. Caught up in the flurry of aerobic contortions, Arthur soon lost track of time. The class it seemed was going slightly faster and a bit longer than the day gone by. His arm-waving faded and his skip-and-a-hop faltered. Pretty good workout,

Arthur: An Actuarial Odyssey

Arthur thought to himself, as he continued to feed himself a steady diet of encouraging clichés. If you want it, ya gotta work for it... no pain no gain, he thought.

By the time members of the class paired up, Arthur's stamina was much depleted. Felicia took Arthur through the paces, sensing his badly weakened and exhausted condition. But this day Felicia seemed a new person. No longer the vengeful, brooding, jilted high school sweetheart, she was a professional aerobics instructor—just doing her job. A renewed confidence now filled Arthur as he marched off to breakfast with the others.

His energies sapped by the invigorating aerobics workout, Arthur returned to his cabin after breakfast to take a quick nap before resuming his activities. When he awoke, Arthur was startled to find he had slept through the entire afternoon. He'd been more tired than he thought. Arthur quickly dressed and hurried along to enjoy that evening's Happy Camper Cruise Line activities. The brochure made the evening's events sound well worth attending—among other treats, this was "Walking the Plank Bungee-Jumping Night."

Several sets of teeth had constructed a quite authentic-looking plank off the port side of the ship. Passengers strapped on the harness and Bungee line and were ordered to "walk the plank," plunging 100 feet into the unforgiving waters below only to have the Bungee cord snap back and lift them high into the air for hours of fun for all. Among the gathered passengers, however, little

Arthur: An Actuarial Odyssey

courage could initially be summoned. And so, Arthur bravely volunteered to start things off.

"Sure, I'll 'walk the plank,'" Arthur assured a waiting set of teeth, as he looked back and giggled with the other passengers.

The teeth readied Arthur. He was handed a safety helmet and made to sign a ten-page liability release so they could "let the fun begin." The teeth ordered Arthur to "walk to plank" for his "unspeakable crimes" and Arthur played along defiantly proclaiming his innocence. The teeth handed out torches and brief scripts to the "surly mob" of cruise line passengers. Arthur snickered as the other passengers demanded that he be "thrown to the sharks!" and "sent to the sea's merciless depths!"

"But I am innocent I tell you! Innocent!" Arthur called out in mock indignation before leaping from the end of the plank.

As a pair of Happy Camper Cruise Line paramedics were later reviving Arthur, he could sense that something had gone wrong. A set of teeth explained that the settings were slightly misaligned and, as a consequence, when the Bungee cord snapped back it had driven him into the side of the ship. Given the remarkable elasticity of the Bungee cord, Arthur had apparently been slammed into the ship's steel hull almost eleven times before coming to rest.

At the same time, up on deck a torch had accidentally started a small fire, averting people's attention from Arthur's fate until someone in the engine room heard the

Arthur: An Actuarial Odyssey

clanging sound. The good news was that after dousing the flames and reeling in Arthur's flaccid body, the teeth were able to readjust the bungee cord and continue with the Happy Camper Cruise Line's scheduled festivities. Arthur retired to his cabin for the evening. sensing the onset of a headache.

The next day, Arthur awoke refreshed and raring to go. He set out on his morning jog, pulling his sweat band snugly over his head bandage. This day, he arrived at his aerobics class just as it began. Felicia opened with some rudimentary jumping jacks. Arthur was working up quite a sweat with the slightly forced pace of the warm-up jumping jacks. But he liked the idea of jump-starting his pulse in the dawn's early light. As with the previous class, the mix of aerobics enthusiasts seemed again somewhat *less* mixed. There was now hardly anyone who was portly or heavy set. Most, in fact, were in top shape. Arthur resolved himself to keep pace.

Felicia led everyone through a host of new aerobics exercises which she said were designed to stimulate all the muscles of the body. The tape deck blared a collection of James Brown's greatest hits and Felicia extended her right arm to the side turning tiny circles. She stretched her left arm over her head, waving it back and forth to the James Brown beat. She then held her right leg straight out in front of her and instructed the class to perform full squats on their remaining left leg. Arthur could feel the workout reaching his every muscle, as Felicia had promised.

Arthur: An Actuarial Odyssey

After ten minutes or so of what Felicia liked to call "Burying the Pelican," she had them hold a full squat for one minute before moving on to the next exercise. The next routine was slightly more difficult. With hands on hip, Felicia began by touching her forehead to the ground in front of her. She then grabbed her left ankle and returned to a standing position, while pulling her left foot to her chest. The exercise was then repeated with the right ankle and so on. Arthur stumbled badly at first. Other's in the class cast him derogatory and disgusted looks of encouragement and he managed to muddle through with a rough equivalent of the intended contortions.

The pace and rigor of the aerobic session had clearly picked up. By the time, Felicia order folks to reunite with their partner, Arthur struggled merely to reunite with several of his limbs. This is a great workout, thought Arthur, as his neck muscles went limp and his head drooped forward. The degree of difficulty continued apace with the paired exercises. As one partner held the other's feet to the deck, the second partner tried to jog in place. Arthur could not budge, with Felicia gripping his feet for a few minutes of weird, anti-erotic convulsions. Felicia then had a much easier time of it, with Arthur bent holding her feet. Her piston-like steps snapped high in the air and Arthur took several knees to the groin before the breakfast bell signaled the end of his daily bout of physical fitness.

After class, Arthur dragged his frail frame to the breakfast table. As he sat sipping his tomato juice, Arthur

Arthur: An Actuarial Odyssey

began to sense that aerobics may not, after all, be for him. Felicia spotted Arthur across the Beaming with Sunshine Breakfast Room deep in contemplation. She stopped by just to assure that Arthur wasn't thinking of skipping out on his aerobics commitment—the same way that he had broken commitments in the past. Arthur promised her that—though a bit frazzled from the workout—nothing could keep him from an early a.m, heart-racing, all-body, aerobics experience. Felicia smiled.

"That's good Arthur. You know the last thing I'd want to face is having to walk into that aerobics class all alone and forlorn, without a partner."

Arthur swallowed hard and awkwardly dug his spoon deep into his cantaloupe.

"No, no don't worry about that. I would never... I mean, I wouldn't... that is..."

"That's what I thought Artie boy. I knew you wouldn't disappoint me. Well, see ya tomorrow."

Arthur passed the day flat on his back by the pool catching some rays and trying to restore his strength and the feeling in his eyebrows. Occasionally, a pair of teeth would pass by but Arthur was too decrepit to summon them. He lounged in this semi-comatose condition on into the dinner hour, when he managed to pull his body from the deck chair to take in the evening meal. His backside was riddled with the indented markings of the deck chair's crisscross pattern.

Arthur: An Actuarial Odyssey

Matters weren't helped by the Happy Camper Cruise Line's thematic dinners. That evening was "Stranded on a Desert Island" night. The teeth were dressed in rags as they served raw crabs with buttered cactus on scraps of drift wood with lukewarm salt water. Arthur left dinner early and went straight to bed, passing on that evening's film—"The Making, Re-Making, and Re-Re-Making of 'The Poseidon Adventure'."

The next morning's alarm momentarily froze Arthur. He ripped his tortured body from bed and headed out for his regular, relaxing jog. Each step tore like a knife through his lower back. Groggy and exhausted, he managed only two and a half feeble laps around the deck before doggedly willing himself on to the waiting aerobics class. He stood in the third row still sleepy and trying to resummon his vim and vigor. It seemed to Arthur that there was yet again something off about the class this morning.

Though he'd had his suspicions for many days, the signs were now unmistakable. Felicia had been systematically weeding out those members of the aerobics class sporting less than stellar physiques, while coaxing a succession of Olympic body builders to join. By now, though almost too horrible to fathom, her plan was clear. Felicia had set in motion a diabolical scheme to aerobics Arthur to death! This would be a murder no detective could trace. She was going to raise her aerobics class to new heights of physical, mental, and gyrational endurance, leaving Arthur's worn and wasted body to rot

Arthur: An Actuarial Odyssey

on deck—just as he had left her lo' those many years ago to spend her prom night all alone and forlorn. Class began with back-flips into a set of hand stand push-ups.

"And a one, and a two, and a three," Felicia called out, as Arthur leaned against a rail for balance, while fumbling with his hand stand push-ups.

But this morning's warm-up routine did not last long and the class moved immediately into an exercise Felicia liked to call "The Bone-Crusher Fall and Bounce." Felicia turned over the tape and began to demonstrate the exercise. She pulled her left foot behind her head and began falling forward, as a recording of Barber's *Adagio for Strings* hauntingly played in the background.

Arthur knew it was now or never. The breakfast bell could not save him this morning. He had to act with swift resolve. Arthur spotted the release line for a row of rescue rafts and gingerly maneuvered his way over—continuing to jiggle and gyrate with aerobic aplomb. He had nearly reached the line without detection when suddenly Felicia switched out from the "The Bone-Crusher Fall and Bounce" exercise and instructed everyone to pair up for the next routine. Felicia searched the class for her wayward partner. Arthur knew this was his last chance. He flew to the raft line, cut one free, and it dropped into the water. His feet disappeared below the bow, as he dove after the raft.

Undeterred, Felicia cried out, "Man over board!" and released a second rescue raft to chase after him.

Arthur: An Actuarial Odyssey

Arthur steadied his wobbly craft and was starting the engine when he heard Felicia's raft drop and saw her spandex leotards slice into the waters. After struggling briefly, Arthur's engine kicked into gear and he made his escape. Arthur skimmed across the water's surface, as his spent body fell back, with one hand racing the engine at full throttle. Meanwhile, Felicia now took control of her craft as well and darted off after Arthur. Arthur's raft skipped along the water with abandon, until the Happy Camper Cruise Line became but a distant speck on the horizon. He saw no sign of Felicia. Feeling free of danger, he cut his engine to reserve fuel and drifted peaceably along, buoyed by the calm sea's gentle waves.

But, before he knew it, Felicia was upon him. She had idled her engine and silently paddled the final half mile to launch a sneak attack. Like all dastardly villains, however, she made one fatal slip. Hers was to scream, "Ah Hah!" just before pouncing. Arthur, recognizing the classic "Ah hah!" line as the clichéd modus operandi of every formulaic, evil, arch enemy, instinctively grabbed a paddle and swung to knock Felicia off her feet. He caught her in the midsection and she doubled over in pain, tumbling to the back of her raft. Arthur pulled the engine's rip cord but he'd twisted it around an oar. Felicia regathered herself to strike again.

"Hah, you thought you could escape me! You thought prom night was behind you forever!"

Felicia reached for Arthur's raft but he managed to push her away with his oar at the last second.

Arthur: An Actuarial Odyssey

"But that was so long ago. We were kids. You couldn't possibly—"

Felicia clawed the edge of Arthur's raft with her oar as the two struggled.

"You humiliated me! You made me look like a fool. You turned me into some kind of monstrous, hideous beast for all the school to laugh at—all alone and forlorn at the prom! Since then, my life has been nothing but a constant memory of the pain and agony of past rejection. Now I must kill the memory!"

Felicia slipped, trying to stand.

"But... but, I truly believed that Bambi had liver cancer. She said she only had a few months to live!"

Arthur struggled to keep her raft at bay.

"Lies! All lies! To think I actually believed that the two of you were innocently looking at cemetery plots all those summer afternoons!"

"But it's true! By the time Bambi and I broke up I was on a first name basis with every mortician in town!"

Felicia was drawing near.

"And so why didn't she die Arthur!?! Get yourself out of that one you shameless cad!"

Felicia's raft was nearly beside his and he knew she meant business. Even as a teenager, Felicia had always lapsed into a stock, 1950's gangster movie dialect when extremely angry.

Arthur: An Actuarial Odyssey

"She'd been lying to me the whole time! I swear, if I had known, none of this would have ever happened—"

Felicia had pulled the two rafts side by side and braced herself to leap into his.

"I'm going to kill you!"

"No, I tell you it was all a misunderstanding! I tell you.."

In the melee Arthur had managed to grab back his oar. He swung wildly, catching Felicia squarely in the back of the head. Her lifeless body collapsed at his feet. In a panic, he rolled her body over the side and watched as it slowly sank to the ocean floor. He collapsed back onto his seat exhausted and drained, as the waves softly smacked the two rafts up against one another. Arthur lay resting momentarily before heading back to the ship.

Just then, a badly decomposed hand appeared to rise from the water and grasp the edge of his raft, pulling Arthur into the water. Arthur struggled mightily with what, at first, he did not know was beast or human. He felt himself dragged further beneath the water's surface before somehow managing to pull free. He swam back to the surface and crawled into his raft. He struggled to start the engine and the raft drifted quietly on the water's calm surface. Suddenly, a tremendous thud threw Arthur from his feet as something, or someone, rammed hard against the bottom of his raft. Arthur desperately pulled the rip cord. Then, there in the water, he caught sight of his

Arthur: An Actuarial Odyssey

terrible foe—an amorphous dark object rising to the surface.

He stood by; his oar at the ready. His mind racing, Arthur imagined Felicia's half-dead zombie returning to slay him. But nothing in Arthur's worst nightmares could have prepared him for what he was about to confront. There, racing to the ocean's surface, seething with rage, consumed by hate, its fierce eyes burning for revenge—it was the dreaded, killer baby seal. And this time, especially given Arthur's sordid fast-food past, it was personal.

Arthur froze as the killer baby seal rammed his small raft, once again knocking him off his feet. Before long, the treacherous waters surrounding his rickety raft were teeming with killer baby seals. They circled his teetering raft, almost toying with him. Arthur had read about the harrowing plight of these baby seals from Arctic lands. Forced to migrate, they had developed the keen instincts of a killer. Whenever, Arthur would lift his oar to strike, two or three killer baby seals would rise from the water and spit at him with a spray of salty sea water. The conniving beasts, Arthur bemoaned.

At last, his engine kicked into gear and he managed to speed off just as the thuggish, killer baby seals were closing in. Breathing a deep sigh of relief, Arthur made haste and raced back to the Happy Camper Cruise Line. After battling Felicia the aerobics instructor to the death and barely escaping the clutches of a wilding gang of killer baby seals, his nerves were on edge, his strength exhausted. Back on board, Arthur returned to the intoxicating comfort of the pampering teeth's hospitality and he did his best to simply lay low for the remainder of the voyage. Once back on dry land, he'd be able to re-think his mission and begin his quest anew.

The Happy Camper Cruise Line reached port two days later. Arthur knew not where. And Arthur cared not where. Here, fate had determined, he would make his new home and continue his search for the meaning and purpose of life. Arthur thanked the many sets of teeth who had gathered, bid them farewell, and embarked upon this new land. Arthur's search would continue—as he would learn—in the trying climate and barbaric, social depravity of some nameless and hopelessly exploited tropical island.

Arthur found himself trapped in a playland of the disgustingly rich—tourist and destination wedding planner alike. Here, Arthur soon surmised, the moneyed few would gather for many a day of sun, beaches, and the wanton exploitation of a proud, native peoples whose simple lives had been turned into mere instruments of pleasure for the pale-skinned, vacationing bourgeoisie or—as he would always add with a gasp—many a corporate retreat.

Arthur: An Actuarial Odyssey

Chapter Fourteen

Arthur took a deep bite from his mango and set out to land some job here or there, presenting himself as just another local, itinerant worker, so that he could observe class struggle more closely. After little luck in his first ten attempts, Arthur decided to change "observe class struggle more closely" to "support wife and five kids" on the application forms. This met with immediate success. Not a week into the rigors of the international tourism industry and already Arthur was learning the ease and convenience of the simple lie. Where this would all lead, Arthur could not say.

Arthur's new life would not be easy. Passing himself off as an indigent mute, Arthur avoided the need to speak and thereby reveal his complete ignorance of the native language. He took the identity of Pedro, the eldest son of a poor peasant family from the hills, who had come in search of a job after many poor harvests. His complimentary Happy Camper Cruise Line t-shirt had

Arthur: An Actuarial Odyssey

nearly undone this fiction. He was able to explain through gestures, however, that he had found the shirt washed up on the shore one day and that—though he understood that it represented a decadent, exploitative global industry that was in many ways responsible for his people's desperate plight—he had no other clean shirt. Most people generally followed Arthur's gestures up to the point of finding it on the beach and then smiled politely.

Arthur's new job was brutal on his back and agony for his knees. The demanding physical labor left Arthur hollow and broken. Behind the boss' back Arthur would gesture to the others that we must organize the workers. Yet, each time, he was badly misunderstood and the others would tell him to simply go and do it in the ocean like everybody else. Arthur's official title was assistant international cuisine sampler. He pushed a cart the length of the beach each day from 8 in the morning until 9 at night selling "tropical flavored" snow-cones.

As the newest member of the crew he would always get the cart with one bad wheel which constantly veered off to the left. Sales were quite slow due to his constant struggle to keep the cart out of the ocean as well as his need to use large, sweeping gestures—rather than shouting out—to hawk his snow-cones to sun bathers lounging 20 to 30 yards down the beach.

Arthur's first few attempts to gesticulate the notion of eating a snow-cone were at first tragically misinterpreted. He would approach a young couple, gesturing excitedly with his hands the cool, refreshing pleasure of eating a

Arthur: An Actuarial Odyssey

delicious snow-cone on the beach. More often than not, however, the couples read Arthur's antics as obscene and profane gestures that sent most fleeing from the beach. For the first few days, the gesticulating figure of Arthur could be seen making his way down the shoreline and leaving a trail of empty beaches behind, as vacationers raced to get away from "that sick pervert with a cart," as he came to be know. Business picked up after Arthur took a different tact and replaced hand gestures with a large sign that he crafted.

While peddling his flavored ice to the bronzing bourgeoisie, Arthur made sure to keep a notepad ever-at-the-ready to record his unnerving observations. Indeed, Arthur felt a close kinship and solidarity with the exploited masses beside whom he labored and this was reflected in many of his notes at day's end. Often, Arthur would focus on the low-level, intra-class warfare he saw waged each day on the island's wave-tossed beaches of iniquity. There were many examples.

I approached a filthy rich couple. They were applying sunscreen to beautify themselves, while completely ignoring the plight of the downtrodden not eight blocks away begging for food in the streets. They saw me approaching and with a haughty wave called me over. With rising pangs of disgust and revulsion I meekly trod over. They asked for a Strawberry Derby—a particular favorite of the upper crust. As I passed it along to

Arthur: An Actuarial Odyssey

> them, I could sense their complete disregard for the working-class.
>
> They tipped me a dollar as if to say, 'There, I've done my part; now go and make something of your life.' I gave my exaggerated appreciation to fulfill my half of the customary, social ritual, bestowing upon them the role of savior for we mere paupers. Heading off, I distinctly heard the word 'riff-raff.' As the beaches were littered with bourgeois couples and families, it was impossible to say which privileged group had made the remark. And so I had no choice but to continue along the beach, peddling my wares—the target of a thousand off-color comments from the sun-drenched leisure class.

At other times Arthur's notes detailed the incessant battles between the workers and the boss man. Like the time Arthur participated in an actual act of food service industry sabotage.

> It was late in the afternoon, on a particularly sultry summer day. I pushed along awash in sweat, my animated sales pitch down to a pitiful, lifeless wave. Up ahead I spotted a fellow snow-cone worker. We stopped to pass the time beneath the sun's torturous rays. My fellow worker was incensed. He'd had a very poor day—few sales

Arthur: An Actuarial Odyssey

and nearly no tips. I shrugged in solidarity. The worker—clearly agitated and dangerously alienated—explained that he was nearing his breaking point. He just didn't see himself with any kind of a future in the business. I put my hand on the worker's scorched shoulder.

"Sometimes I feel as if I just want to throw my cart into the ocean and be done with it," the worker confessed.

I smiled, gesturing dramatically that I too had such thoughts.

"So why don't we—damn it! What stops us!?!"

I sensed that the worker was dead serious. Surveying over my shoulder and down the stretch of beach, I gestured back, "Right, why don't we?"

"Hey! I'll race you!" he shouted, barreling toward the sea with his bouncing cart of snow-cones.

"Wait!" I gestured. In hot pursuit, my cart swerving badly to the left, I tried to keep up with my revolting co-worker. I raced along the beach, the sand gripping my toes, the sea breeze rushing through my hair. It was as if time stood still, as if all moved in slow motion. I laughed wildly, feeling free and alive, hurdling toward the sea

Arthur: An Actuarial Odyssey

with my livelihood alongside my deranged colleague. The beach's startled Fortune 500 sunbathers turned with faint care to stare down our class-riven tomfoolery. The rolling waves moved across the water, the white foam breaking high in the air against the blue sky.

I knew there was no turning back, no time for regrets, no voice inside my head to summon the usual dry, suffocating, middle class inhibitions—challenging the propriety of such a moment. Sometimes, I thought to myself—as my cart skipped along the sand—affirming one's solidarity with the working class can be so liberating, so up-lifting; ultimately obliterating those stifling social prohibitions against a single, desperate act. Just then, my cart caught a bump along the beach and flew high into the air, stopping just short of the water's edge. The momentum threw me headlong over the mangled cart and into the rolling waves. I came to rest near my fellow worker who sat beside his half-submerged snow-cone cart. We looked to one another without speaking. At last, if but for a moment, I was one with the working class and I had my overturned snow-cone cart just up the beach to prove it.

Other notes further suggested a smoldering desire for organized class struggle among the workers.

Arthur: An Actuarial Odyssey

Today I have come across what appears to be a smoldering desire for organized class struggle among the workers. Around noon I returned to the snow cone cart repair shop to oil my wheels. I found the mechanics in heated debate. A senior mechanic had just been fired and it seemed that the others were planning a large, potentially volatile, protest march on the boss' office. They were drawing up their demands. In a show of extreme democratic principles each mechanic seemed to be writing up their own list of demands, presumably to be combined with the others in the end. Soon, I had to get back to the beach where, I told the mechanics, I would help spread word of their noble cause among the laboring masses.

Each of the mechanics then went out themselves and shared their demands with the workers along the beach. The movement was building rapidly and one could sense a percolating militancy engulfing the beaches just days before the planned march. The mechanics stayed on the job, defiantly working—it seemed—with a new mission, a new resolve. I approached one of the mechanics to discuss the movement's progress. His response at first confused me and I assumed that, for the sake of the movement, discretion on the part of the mechanic's inner circle was imperative.

"So how's it going?" I gestured.

"I'm feeling good. I'm feeling good," he assured.

"So you're confident we can win?" I gestured.

"We?"

"The workers. Your victory will be a victory for all workers," I gestured.

"Oh, the workers. Sure I suppose."

"So listen," I continued, "You don't have to give me any details, but are there any surprises planned?"

The mechanic appeared confused at first. Playing it cool, I assured myself.

"What kind of surprises?" he wryly asked.

"You know," I gestured, "maybe a slow-down, a strike—anything."

"Do you really think the other workers would back me with such a move?"

"Your victory is our victory, you defeat is our defeat," I gestured back.

"Do you really think the workers feel that way?" the increasingly excited mechanic asked.

Arthur: An Actuarial Odyssey

"Take my word for it, the boss messes with you and he'll have all of us to answer to," I gestured.

I could see the mechanic was impressed. We shook hands and parted.

The next day the mechanics marched on the boss' office. I had convinced about four or five snow cone-cart pushers who had been waiting for repairs to join the movement in a selfless act of defiance. Still intimidated by the watchful eye and vengeful hand of the boss man, the others feared joining me in my chants and protest songs. So the seven of us purposely marched to the office in silence, as I militantly gestured to anyone who could see us. When we reached the office the mechanics disappeared inside, returning my clenched fist salute with slightly confused looks—apparently not wanting to let on to the boss man.

We waited in solidarity a full five minutes for their triumphant return. I leaped from my seat as the office door flew open. The mechanics filed out. Their mood was glum. One of the mechanics, however, was quite ebullient. I approached my comrade to learn the details. It seems that, what on the surface had appeared to be a militant act of worker struggle in the face of an unjustly discarded colleague, had in fact been an overt campaign of open competition for the fired mechanic's supervisor position. How blind I had

Arthur: An Actuarial Odyssey

been. The other snow-cone cart pushers, whose class consciousness I had carefully cultivated and who stood at the ready to help in "the struggle," must have been devastated. I watched as they somberly followed the mechanics back to the repair shop.

"Be strong," I gestured to them, "Keep the faith."

Most tragic however, was to be the fate of the unfortunate mechanic with whom I had strategized. Passed over for the promotion, but confident he had the full backing of the workers—due to our ill-conceived, side conversation—he pressed for a mass strike. A few days later, when the masses inexplicably disregarded his call, he was fired after setting up his one-person picket line. It would seem that I may have woefully misread what appeared to be the tell-tale signs of revolution in the air. I must study more carefully the ways of the workers here. I must go live among the squalid and redouble my efforts.

Arthur's needs were few. He moved to a rooming house in a desperately poor section of the city. There, among the squalor and the filth, among the downtrodden and the abandoned, Arthur shared his life with others who had come in search of bettering their lot. Arthur's four-foot by eight-foot room had a single small window

Arthur: An Actuarial Odyssey

looking out into an alleyway where the pimps and drug dealers peddled their trade. Arthur would sit by the window ledge each night, playing his harmonica and commiserating with the forlorned and forgotten, until a guiding voice or purposeful gunshot would let him know it was time to "turn that fucking light out" on another day.

The boarding house was home to a rag-tag collection of migrant workers who had made their way from distant lands and distant lives. These were hard-working, hard-living men—the kind who earned their keep by the sweat of their brow. The kind who relied on protective walls to guard their emotions, short-tempers to stem their boiling frustrations, and physical violence to lessen the legal entanglements of protracted, statutory, conflict resolution. Yes, thought Arthur, these were real men. Perhaps the kind of real men that Arthur's father had hoped he would be. And deep down, Arthur knew, the kind of real man he had always secretly wanted himself to be. Arthur felt he could identify with these men—their pain, their anger, their emerging, revolutionary class consciousness.

Sitting on the stoop outside the boarding house one evening, just hanging with a few of the guys, Arthur got a pretty good sense of the life these men were living. After a long day's work, Arthur came along and discovered the others in what appeared at first to be deep examination of the vexing conditions of the international working-class.

"We can deny it no longer, they have abandoned us," lamented Raúl.

Arthur: An Actuarial Odyssey

"When we have always been there for them," added Carlos.

"And at such a critical moment," gestured Arthur, flittering his arms about in disgust.

"So what did you really expect?" asked Raúl rhetorically.

"I say we go ahead without them. We cannot let the laziness of a few spoil it for everyone," Carlos insisted.

Arthur gestured that, trying as it may be from time to time, solidarity was critical within the struggle and that they must wait it out for the sake of the movement.

Ignoring Arthur, Carlos went alone to the store for a pack of cigarettes, refusing to wait any longer for the others. Arthur was relieved to have misconstrued the conversation and sat beside a contemplative Raúl. The two shared a profound silence. Arthur patiently allowed Raúl to gather his thoughts.

"You know what I've been thinking?" Raúl began.

Arthur braced himself. Raul was in his mid-40's. The lines creasing his face and worn, calloused hands reflected the punishing life of deprivation he had known over his four decades. His raspy, deliberate voice bespoke a life marked by disappointment and despair. Indeed, Raúl had led an almost uniquely tragic life. He was a chronically unemployed ski instructor from a mountainous region of the interior where it had not snowed for over four centuries. Such a drought may have

Arthur: An Actuarial Odyssey

broken a lesser person. But Raúl—passionate about skiing since early childhood—was a survivor. Ever faithful to his dreams, he carried his ski equipment with him everywhere, not wanting to risk missing that first flake. Raúl now leaned forward, adjusting his ski cap.

"I'm starting to have doubts," Raúl admitted.

Arthur gave a broad, reassuring smile and gestured that everyone had doubts from time to time. The important thing was that we do our best each day, remind ourselves just how special each and every one of us truly is, and try to avoid towers and high-powered rifles. Arthur couldn't believe the sappy sentiment he was spewing with his hands. But try as he might nothing but cliché after cliché kept rolling off his ten fingers.

"Yes, yes, we've all seen you gesture those thoughts a million times. And I'm sure in your own way—they must actually mean something to you. But I—what? No, no, I don't need a friendship hug."

Arthur sat back down.

"I guess what I'm trying to say is… Well, lately I've been having these dreams. They're kind of off the wall, a little bizarre… anyway they're probably nothing."

Arthur gestured Raúl to go on.

"Well, alright. Generally, it's actually the same dream. It starts out with me standing on an assembly line in a huge factory. There's thousands of machines going. I'm working all fine and everything when all of a sudden I notice there's no other people working there. They're all robots. So I try to go to the other side of the factory to find someone. But when I try to walk I can't. My arms and legs are made out of metal and it turns out that I'm a robot too."

Arthur gestured, "Wow!"

"After struggling a bit I usually wake up in a cold sweat."

Arthur gestured, "How remarkably Kafkaesque."

"But what do you think it could mean? Am I simply going insane?" Raúl asked in hushed tones, loosening the shoulder strap on his ski pouch.

Arthur reminded Raúl with his gestures that sanity was no substitute for personality and, as such, had never been a particular goal of his. With respect to the possible meaning of such a dream, Arthur gestured that it was, of course, pure speculation but that he had a few thoughts. First, he wanted to know the color of the robots.

"They were gray-metallic," said Raúl.

"And what they were making in the factory?" Arthur gestured.

"I can't be certain. But I believe we were making shackles to fit around people's ankles."

"Ok, ok, I'm getting a mental image," Arthur gestured. Arthur could sense that this was a highly symbolic dream.

Arthur: An Actuarial Odyssey

But what could this imagery mean? Arthur contemplated a good, long while when suddenly it struck him.

"I've got it!" gestured Arthur, excitedly cupping his hands to form a light bulb over his head.

"What, what is it? What could it mean?" Raúl asked.

Arthur gestured that he, of course, was no expert, but that in his opinion it seemed clear that Raúl secretly wanted to kill his father so he could "be with" his mother.

There being no *subtle* way of gesturing "be with," Raúl grabbed a ski pole and chased after Arthur cursing and vowing to kill him. Eventually Raúl cooled off and Arthur gestured that indeed, upon reflection, he had another interpretation. The two sat panting heavily, as Carlos returned.

"We'll continue this later," Raúl whispered.

"Sure thing," replied Arthur through heavily hyperventilated hand motions.

"Here ya are," said Carlos, as he threw Raul a pack of cigarettes. "Hey, Pedro, I got some good news for you."

"What's up?" gestured Arthur.

"I saw that guy I told you about—Miguel. Looks like you're in luck. That drug bust got screwed up. Two guys from the projects took it in the chest and they took out one undercover narc. So they're gonna be lookin' for a new dishwasher down at The Bistro. You just have to go

Arthur: An Actuarial Odyssey

down and talk to Miguel. Your days of pushing that busted cart along the beach are over."

Arthur gestured that he hadn't wanted to get the job "this way."

"Sure, sure, but look," said Carlos, "it's like you're always saying, it's the law of the jungle." With these last remarks, Carlos mimicked Arthur's hand gestures depicting a gazelle being robbed at gun point by a rabbit.

Arthur began his new life as a dishwasher the next day. Carlos had landed Arthur a gig in a pretty ritzy part of town, a real high class joint. From four in the afternoon till one in the morning Arthur stood up to his elbows in suds, the steam rising from the water, and his shirt drenched in sweat and lavender scrubbing bubbles. All the while, the furious pace of satisfying the bourgeoisie's rapacious appetite kept the kitchen a hectic hellscape of activity.

"Leg of lamb for table three!" someone would call out.

"Filet mignon on nine!" another would yell.

"Where's my lasagna!?! For God's sake, where's my lasagna!?!"

Arthur continued his scouring in disgust. It was almost too much for him to bear; the spectacle of human beings driven at a pace that would break a team of horses. The restaurant's sinister, inner workings captured the cold, naked truth of class struggle, as few other hellscapes could, Arthur thought to himself. It was all a cruel,

Arthur: An Actuarial Odyssey

unspeakable outrage. At five each afternoon the bourgeoisie would begin poking through the window making certain all was being readied for their five-thirty feeding. By five-twenty-nine they were lined three or four deep at the door. Waiters and waitresses took their stations. The chefs stood, ladle at the ready. Bus boys adjusted their bow ties. Arthur peered out from behind his suds. The doors opened and in rushed the famished bourgeoisie. Each of the restaurant's hives had their role.

The chefs, chained by the bourgeoisie's gluttonous appetite to their boiling cauldrons and steaming ovens, kept pace with a sturdy determination. Forced to make due with less space than the master bathrooms for most of their money-drenched customers, they hovered over their sautéed masterpieces with the care of skilled surgeons. These were seasoned professionals. They'd been trained to withstand the most barbaric of conditions. When the kitchen ran low on parsley they alternated garnishing as if it was child's play. When the pace of the bourgeoisie's bottomless demands grew too great they took things to another level.

The wait staff, meanwhile, occupied two contesting worlds of struggle and merriment created by and for the service industry. While circulating among the engorged, filthy-rich customers in humble service, the wait staff pleasured others with plastic smiles and hollow laughs. Their good cheer and prostituted emotions were base occupational requisites. On returning to the netherworld (or kitchen), their smiles reverted to revulsion, their

Arthur: An Actuarial Odyssey

laughs became quiet shrieks. Arthur watched this unholy transformation night after night. He knew a person's breaking point was merely a matter of time.

At the lowest rung were the bus boys. The bus boys' task—arguably an impossible ask—was to clear as rapidly as possible the table scraps and discarded instruments of engorgement left by one set of the bourgeoisie to prepare for the arrival of the next set. Their white aprons and gray, plastic bins darted about the dining room; always a half step behind the departing bourgeoisie and one step ahead of those newly commanding a table. Their return to the kitchen was simply a blur, stopping only to off their load beside the sink for Arthur to sort.

The rhythm of the kitchen was dictated by the whims of bourgeois tastes. If the rolls weren't warm enough, the drinks not stirred but mixed, the appetizer not suited to the mercurial discernment of the propertied public, Arthur knew the entire operation could crumble. He stood scrubbing dishes night after night, observing this full tragic comedy unfold.

Orchestrating the entire operation were the henchmen of the bourgeoisie—mid-level managers. They were too good to be associated with the likes of we mere workers, Arthur noticed, and yet too uncultured to occupy the celestial social circles of their bourgeois masters. These were masterful ideological contortionists whose lives were torn by their selfless service to a class of persons wholly unaccepting of their less-than-country-club-style

Arthur: An Actuarial Odyssey

upbringings. Spit on by the bourgeoisie even as they blanched reflexively at the sight of an unpolished spoon, this mutant class form could do nothing but take their frustrations out on the hapless workers a rung beneath them.

Arthur winced whenever hearing that vainglorious laughter of the bourgeoisie at the sight of acrimony between mid-level manager and worker. More a chortle then a chuckle, it was as if to say, "Hah, the mindless plebeian masses! They are so easily divided! Our reign over them shall not ever end so long as we retain our omnipotent power to declare a roll not warm, a utensil unclean, or a meal not to our taste!" Arthur's fists clenched and he let out a low, intemperate moan at the sound of that distinct cackle coming from the dining room.

As the dishwasher, Arthur was always among the last to leave at evening's end. One night, while gathering his things from the locker, Arthur overheard two managers speaking in hushed, serious tones in the main dining room. He discretely moved behind a door to listen further and became quite excited by their words.

Arthur's loose interpretation of their conversation was that—for the first time it seemed—these managers were questioning the underlying class structure protected by an oppressive, alienating societal facade. They were wondering if their own material interests did not, indeed, lay with the oppressed working masses upon whose neck they kept their heel as their bourgeois taskmasters ordered. Arthur wanted to step out from behind the partition, confirm their suspicions, and give them both a big friendship hug. But for now he could only listen in silence.

"More coffee, Guillermo?"

"Sure why not," Guillermo replied, a desperate resignation flattening his voice.

"Quite a night, huh, quite a night."

"Yep, quite a night."

Arthur pictured the two of them seething with rage—two burning infernos ready to lash out at the system.

"My feet are killing me."

"Yeah, mine too."

Arthur could feel their pain and understood, only too well, just how quickly it could be translated into a powerful blow for revolutionary justice.

"Well, gotta be going."

"Yeah, better be going."

Their boiling frustration and gnawing desperation were but inches from the two men's red-hot surfaces. Arthur knew it was time to act. He leaped out, gesturing wildly to the startled keepers of the bourgeois social order.

"Oh hey Pedro, I didn't know you were still around."

Arthur: An Actuarial Odyssey

Arthur gestured that he had overheard their dispirited, revolutionary longings and he was prepared to lead them in battle against their bourgeois masters.

Not fully grasping, Guillermo replied, "That's fine, just make sure all the dishes are at least soaking."

Arthur rhetorically gestured back, "What are a few dirty dishes in the face of decades of oppression?"

Guillermo reminded Arthur to hit the light on his way out and the two disappeared into the night. Arthur sensed this little playground of the super-rich he had stumbled upon was very nearly ready to explode. Sensing the peoples' frustration, the masses' complete sense of desperate deprivation, Arthur set out to lead the people in revolutionary struggle to defeat the bourgeois enemy and create a true worker's island paradise—free of class struggle, free of all forms of alienation, and free of all unfree things more generally.

Chapter Fifteen

Arthur went home that night and rededicated himself to the movement. He developed flyers to pass along to restaurant workers the next day and called for a mass meeting the very next week. Arthur's message met with skepticism at first. The flyer itself was problematic. Given Arthur's less than complete mastery of the native tongue, he was forced to draw stick figures to animate his message of class struggle. The workers politely looked over his flyers but most were left clueless about the final frame portraying one group of stick figures standing triumphantly over another group of stick figures. Arthur needed better tools to reach his audience.

Consequently, the mass worker's meeting was sparsely attended. Only about six or seven of the "masses" showed up and even they seemed to have misunderstood the meeting's purpose. Each had brought masts from sailing boats, expecting a repair class for those "struggling" with difficult mast problems. Arthur

Arthur: An Actuarial Odyssey

was demoralized but not defeated by these early setbacks. Pushing forward, he rejiggered the misconstrued meeting for sailboat mast repair to deliver his message of class struggle more pointedly. The worker's listened and came to better understand. After his inspiring words, one worker stepped forward to ask further questions. His name was Julio and he would become Arthur's right hand in the forging of a movement.

In a short period, Julio fully dedicated himself to the cause. Each night he and Arthur could be seen conspiring over coffee in a discreet café or reviewing the revolution's logistics on a secluded park bench. At long last, the movement was taking off. With Arthur at the helm and Julio navigating their course, Arthur knew victory was just a matter of time. Julio reworked the flyers and the two held a series of meetings among small circles of workers rather than initially holding mass events. The two sensed a real enthusiasm for revolution among the workers. Many left the meetings offering to lend their complete support by not telling anyone where they had been or what they had discussed.

After several weeks the movement mushroomed. Over 500 workers across the island had agreed to not tell anyone about anything. Arthur felt it was no longer safe for he and Julio to meet openly in public settings. It was time to take the movement underground. From then on, to throw off any suspicions, Julio was only to be identified as Comandante Zero and Arthur would be known simply as Generalissimo. They would meet in remote motel

Arthur: An Actuarial Odyssey

rooms, select safe houses and—were there an emergency—the breakfast cereal aisle of Wagner's grocery and watch repair shop.

Those new to the movement were asked, "do you know what time it is?" The proper response was, "I'm cuckoo for Cocoa Puffs." Tragically, given the ubiquity of this question as a general point of information throughout one's day, great confusion often resulted from the Cocoa Puffs reply and often both persons simply wandered away apologetic and bewildered. Subsequently, the order was altered so that "I'm cuckoo for Cocoa Puffs" became the initial greeting and "do you know what time it is?" served as the reply.

In fact, Arthur and Julio had worked out a complex communications system involving different brand name cereals and directives for the movement when meeting in the grocery aisle. Each brand represented a different place, person, or action. For example, if Julio wanted Arthur to go with him to meet the rubber workers in a church, he would merely first select the Cheerios, then the Frosted Flakes, and, finally, the Raisin Bran, as Arthur watched. They thus communicated by simply picking a series of breakfast cereals without speaking or gesturing to one another. In fact, the entire movement was nearly brought to its knees one week by a late Rice Crispies delivery.

Meanwhile, the workers grew increasingly impatient. The tell-tale signs were everywhere. An average island-wide absentee rate of 22.8% had skyrocketed to 23.4% in

Arthur: An Actuarial Odyssey

just the last three weeks. A virtual sick-out had spontaneously taken hold, when a flu epidemic *coincidentally* hit the island right after one of Arthur and Julio's "message to the workers" pamphlets had encouraged all workers to "take their own temperatures" to see if they were "hot enough" to join the revolutionary movement. The workers were plainly in revolt. They yearned for decisive action and looked to their steadfast leaders for inspiration and direction.

Arthur and Julio determined that now was the time to take refuge in the surrounding hills where they built their remote mountain base camp. They scavenged for materials in town to build a crude radio transmitter and began sending their revolutionary message back to the workers. Arthur, with his long winter in a desolate cabin to steel him, survived life in the mountains quite well. For Julio, it was his dedication and loyalty that proved sufficient to sustain him through the difficult hardships of revolutionary struggle. Each morning Julio would wake the workers—at least those who had their radios on and tuned to the relatively weak frequency of their broadcasts in the early a.m. hours—with his revolutionary message for the day.

Julio had grown enormously in the past few weeks under Arthur's strict-yet-firm tutelage. He'd been transformed from a part-time airport baggage handler into a full-time lieutenant in the worker's movement. His daily radio messages alone, Arthur assured him, were often all that fed the spirits of a beleaguered working class, often left dismayed and demoralized by the, at times, plodding pace of the revolutionary movement. Julio's fidelity to the cause was unsurpassed.

Though Arthur's initial efforts to compose a folk song about Julio failed miserably due to an inability to block out the melody of "Old MacDonald's Farm," Arthur assured Julio that once the revolution took hold he would commission a mighty songstress to write the perfect tune. Julio would give only a modest grin when Arthur spoke of such things, suggesting that such extravagances were unnecessary and that, as they had discussed, a simple statue in St. Julio Park would suffice.

The two were going over plans for the design of St. Julio Park and precisely where to place the Revolutionary St. Julio Water Slide when a clandestine courier approached. He called out the secret revolutionary worker's greeting from a few hundred yards away and "I'm cuckoo for Cocoa Puffs!" echoed through the valley. The two scurried down the path to meet their comrade, hollering back, "do you know what time it is?"

It was Alejandro from the plastics division of the Acme Tool Company. He brought word of a rumored crackdown on revolutionary activities on the island. His informants told him that if Arthur and Julio continued to incite the workers to "rise up and crush the instruments of capitalist oppression" using stationery stolen from the Department of Motor Vehicles they would face substantial fines and potential fraud charges. Arthur's thunderous laugh filled the mountain valley.

Arthur: An Actuarial Odyssey

"And if they fine us, do you know what we shall do?" Arthur gestured, smiling at Julio.

"What?" Alejandro asked.

"We'll delay payment," Arthur smugly replied crossing his arms and grinning off into the distance.

Julio leaped in the air screaming, "Yes, for the workers! We will risk our very creditworthiness!"

"That's right," Arthur gestured.

A stunned Alejandro stood silently agog.

"You see my brother," Julio explained to Alejandro, "When you are dedicated to the worker's struggle there is no price too high, no cost too great. And so, even at substantial personal risk of indebtedness, Generalissimo and I must demonstrate to the workers our willingness to make any sacrifice, no matter how inconvenient for our accustomed lifestyles."

Alejandro knew he was hearing the words of true revolutionaries and simply asked, "And what shall I tell the people?"

Arthur began to gesture. Julio, whose mind now worked in tandem with that of Arthur's, provided a simultaneous interpretation.

"You may tell them that Generalissimo and Comandante Zero—who have all these weeks selflessly labored without food, without electricity, without water, with only the unshakable faith of the workers to sustain them—now must also endure the watchful eye of a sadistic Department of Motor Vehicles run amok with their hired henchmen, flooding the courts with lawsuits, injunctions, and other unspeakable, counter-revolutionary, legal proceedings. But through it all, we remain unfazed, undaunted—in fact we do not even know the meaning of the word 'daunt'—and unrelenting in our commitment to see this movement through to our people's glorious victory."

"This I shall tell to all the people," Alejandro assured.

"Good. Be strong soldier. With you, go the hopes and dreams of all the workers."

Alejandro appeared humbled by Arthur's inspiring words and dashed back down the mountain to deliver the revolutionary message. Days passed. Arthur and Julio continued with their strategizing and daily radio messages to the workers.

At last, the hour came. Arthur was convinced that the workers' revolutionary consciousness had matured, that the movement's final preparations had been readied, and that the bourgeois standard-bearers of the oppressive social order had been sufficiently divided by their heated strategy squabbles—some preferring the use of legal court proceedings and others a low-key campaign of benign neglect to crush the workers. He was prepared to call upon the workers to rise up, take to the streets, and defeat their fat and happy class enemies.

Arthur: An Actuarial Odyssey

As revolutionary ferment blistered, Julio's daily messages grew ever more provocative. This led to a greater focus on the station's programming. He refused to sell anymore advertising time. The movement's sponsors were furious. A-John, a personal soap bar company which had re-packaged it's product as "the soap of the revolutionary worker on the run," threatened to take their advertising money to the movement's sworn class enemies. Frantic Phil's, a Chevrolet dealership which had nearly tripled its sales with its "You Say You Want a Revolution" ad campaign, threatened to give its workers overtime the night of the revolution, badly diminishing the movement's numbers. But Julio was unbending. For the movement every minute was critical when communicating with the workers.

Arthur's cooking show was cut in half, while Julio's movie reviews were radically scaled back. From then on it would be a straight, revolutionary radio format, 24 hours a day. They did not have precise figures for the station's audience share but, as "the voice of the working people," Julio just assumed that he had the ear of all laborers of conscience. His message in the final days before the uprising was simple. First, he would reiterate that there were times in all person's lives when the oppressive conditions of the age, the barbaric cruelty of the hour, the inhuman suffering of the moment called upon each to take action—even at great personal sacrifice. Then he would assure them that this was such

Arthur: An Actuarial Odyssey

an age, this was that hour, and soon would come the moment.

An undeclared war was raging, Julio proclaimed. The factories were the battlefields. The bourgeoisie's managers were the generals. Time cards and poverty wages were the weapons. Members of the exploited and alienated working class were among the casualties. Now, at last, the working class had its own army. Under the command of Generalissimo and Comandante Zero, the downtrodden masses were becoming ripened for liberation. The hour of its rising to crush its bourgeois masters was very much at hand.

Arthur congratulated Julio for putting together a far more upbeat message than he had put out when they first reached their encampment. Back in those days, the movement's prospects were less certain and Julio, new to revolutionary politics, had at first struggled with his messaging. He described the worker's bourgeois bosses as "filthy, stinking rich guys with a lot of filthy, stinking money, wearing filthy, stinking rich clothes, who don't seem at all to like the workers." The oppressive conditions of the workplace were characterized as "a very difficult and not good environment to concentrate on one's work." Julio painted revolutionary class struggle itself as "the brutality and violence of professional wrestling but without a ref there to provide impartiality." Julio had surely grown from those early days.

Arthur was now confident that the movement merely awaited his word and at his call it would to roll forward

Arthur: An Actuarial Odyssey

and quickly seize power. He and Julio discussed the plans for insurrection down to the final details. Arthur and Julio would climb down the south side of the mountain where the two would board a waiting boat in the bay. Julio would sneak ashore near a small fishing village where—via his radio messages—he had arranged for a large cache of weapons. Julio—the mere sight of whom the two were convinced would inspire the worker's to revolutionary action—would organize an army and move on the capitol after passing along word of the uprising to neighboring towns.

Meanwhile, Arthur would circle the island in the boat and station himself just off the coast. There he would await Julio's signal announcing the revolution's glorious success and calling for his triumphant return to lead from the new worker's presidential palace.

Arthur sat with Julio beneath a large tree with branches as bold and brash as these two men. Both knew that this would perhaps be their last chance to speak before raising the flag of victory over the presidential palace. Arthur took a pebble from the ground and flung it off into the distance. Julio grasped his hands behind his head and leaned back on a clump of dirt.

"The night is still," Arthur gestured.

"Indeed," Julio replied.

"It is said that on the night before a revolution, when the air is calm, it is because all of the workers are concentrating so hard on their important roles that they become nervous and spend much time in the bathroom," Arthur gestured.

"My teacher is most wise."

"Yes, I have heard that there have been studies—done secretly, of course, the government would never want such information to leak out—."

"Of course."

"But these studies show a direct connection between low municipal water pressure and general social discontent."

"If this is so, than under Generalissimo's rule all of the people shall always enjoy the highest water pressure ever!"

"Yes, more important than the trains running on time, we must be sure always to keep the rivers flowing."

"Wait, wait—let me write that down." Julio reached for a pen and pad of paper from his bag. He had collected bits of the Generalissimo's thoughts since their setting up camp.

"And that's not all," Arthur continued, sensing an inspiration.

"Go on, Generalissimo, gesture! Gesture and I shall dictate."

"Many have often asked if when a worker is sent to work alone in the forest and there is no one there to see him or her work—are they exploited?"

Arthur: An Actuarial Odyssey

"Yes teacher, we have taken many phone calls about this very topic on our radio call-in show."

"After much study, we have concluded that such a worker is indeed exploited!"

"And what is your rationale teacher?"

"Rationale? Oh yes, the rationale? Well, you see the worker is exploited in such a case because—even though no one can see them actually being exploited—they are among trees. And trees are part of a very complex ecosystem. They give off oxygen and take in carbon dioxide from people."

"Go on teacher."

"So... if a worker is being exploited they, you know, have to breathe more heavily. Hence, they take in more oxygen, give off more carbon dioxide. Therefore, the trees grow faster. Indeed, one will always find the biggest, strongest trees in those areas of the forest where the workers were most exploited."

"Incredible, truly incredible. Definitive proof for one of the workers' oldest philosophical dilemmas."

"This is why deforestation is so feared by the workers."

"I don't follow," Julio said, looking up from his notepad.

"It's a self-defeating exercise from the perspective of the worker. They are cutting down their very source for breathing. For every tree that falls, their capacity to keep working diminishes just that much."

"True genius. We shall need revolutionary, environmental policies to insure the prosperity of our revolutionary worker's state," Julio implored.

"That's right, we shall not repeat the ecological disasters of previous revolutionary movements which sacrificed the workers for a few trees," Arthur gestured.

"And all because they had believed that if a worker were alone in the forest with no one to see them, that they could not be exploited."

"Exactly," Arthur added.

"So Generalissimo," Julio began, changing the subject, "… about tomorrow."

"Yes?"

"You are confident we shall win?"

"As confident as I am that the sun will rise… that birds will take flight… or that the taste of honey will remain sweet. Have you, at this hour, yet lingering doubts? Speak to me of any reservations."

"No, no it's nothing."

"Go on Comandante Zero. Within the movement we must be faultlessly frank."

"Well, alright. There have been a few developments which admittedly make me uneasy."

Arthur: An Actuarial Odyssey

"Go on…"

"Well, to begin with, I found it disappointing that, given the eclectic, revolutionary format we developed for our radio programming, our top-rated show continued to be Automotive Inquiry. Even when we 'opened the lines' for the workers to 'speak their minds' on topics of their choice, the calls were running 9 to 1 for engine trouble over building revolutionary cadre."

"Indeed, for quite a while this had me worried, as well. But now, on the eve of revolution, permit me to assuage your concerns."

"What is it?"

"You see, I figured this out only a few days ago. I hadn't said anything because we have been so busy with the plans. You see, from time to time, there are moments in struggle when the revolutionary masses are actually ahead of their leadership. At such times it is important for the leadership to allow the natural ferment of revolutionary struggle to develop in its own way."

"I don't understand."

"You see, all those calls asking about engine repair were, in fact, nothing but disguised metaphors for building a revolutionary movement. The workers dared not ask such questions directly and so they simply coded their words. Cadre-building became 'head gasket repair,' raising class consciousness became 'fan belt maintenance,' the dangers of workplace spies became 'fuel line problems.'"

"How could I have been so dimwitted!?!"

"Don't give it another thought. As I say, it is only something I came to understand a few days ago. Until then I had the same concerns as you. But what else? Are there other developments causing you doubts?" Arthur gestured.

"Well, to be honest, I took it as a bad sign when we asked the workers, in a show of revolutionary solidarity last Tuesday, to meet that evening with candles in the Plaza and spell out 'Forward to Revolution' but instead they came together and spelled out 'God Bless Our Law and Order President, You Commie Thugs'."

"Again, this was a message one could easily misinterpret," Arthur gestured. "Clearly, however, the lesson to be learned was that they were hearing our message and they were responding."

"But was not their response an unqualified rejection?"

"On the surface yes. But there are many ways to understand, 'God Bless Our Law and Order President, You Commie Thugs. ' You are simply jumping to the worst possible conclusion."

"What is your conclusion?"

"Simple. The workers are frightened. They knew that if they went to the Plaza and returned a revolutionary message, the authorities would move to crush them. And so they composed the most counter-revolutionary message they could think of to get it past the authorities, while still getting a message out to us. The fact of the matter is that, under the circumstances, 'God Bless Our Law and Order President, You Commie Thugs' was nothing less than a spirited, revolutionary call to bring down the established capitalist order."

"Again, I am humbled by the genius of your insight."

"Now, now, we all have our doubts from time to time. What is important is that we not allow surface-level developments and outward appearances to challenge the logical construction of our revolutionary, theoretical outlook and our superior understanding of the underlying worker's consciousness."

"Onward to the worker's revolution!"

"Onward to the worker's revolution!"

Arthur and Julio raised their fists in the air and gestured in unison.

Chapter Sixteen

The next morning the two woke just before five. Arthur looked to Julio. Julio looked to Arthur. Without a word or even a gesture the two stood. Gathering provisions, Julio filled his backpack and prepared to break camp. Arthur looked out over the still sleeping capitol below. By nightfall, he thought to himself, it would belong to the workers as he himself would assure from the presidential palace. Julio motioned to Arthur. Arthur nodded and they were off.

With gazelle-like agility, the two determined revolutionaries descended along the steep, mountain terrain. By dawn, the two had reached the dunes below and cut a path to the waiting boat. The two boarded, pulled in the rope line, and motored out across the bay. Thus far, there was no one in sight and all proceeded as planned. They kept the engines low and managed without lights until well off shore.

Almost 100 yards out and the quiet fishing village now in view, Arthur looked to Julio. This was the spot.

Arthur: An Actuarial Odyssey

The two had not spoken a word since waking. Arthur gave a simple nod. That was enough. Before Arthur had time to even gesture "good luck," Julio dove beneath the clear water's surface. Soon he would awaken the workers, raise an army to take the capitol, and radio Arthur to come ashore to lead the freed masses.

Arthur, however, found himself battling a sea whose waves proved more rough than usual. A storm must have struck further off the coast. Arthur struggled mightily to keep his boat on course. Inspired by thoughts of the worker's heroic fight back at the capitol, Arthur held life and limb together. He was only slightly off course, as he rounded the eastern end of the island back towards the capitol. Having survived the seas fierce tussle, Arthur resolved to have the boat displayed in a worker's museum as a testimony to the great obstacles overcome in the people's heroic revolutionary victory. As Arthur worked on the precise phrasing for a placard beside the exhibit, Julio was just reaching the village square.

Julio did not know exactly what kind of greeting to expect. He most feared that a grand and boisterous celebration would spontaneously break out upon his being spotted. This could delay his vital mission—for which every second was critical. Julio was in luck. The masses proved themselves an exceedingly disciplined army of workers. Not only was there no unseemly celebration compromising the mission's schedule; but, in fact, everyone was keeping things very low key regarding the whole revolution—all was going according to script.

Arthur: An Actuarial Odyssey

Julio was impressed. It was clear that the local workers did not want to alert the authorities to the true powder keg they were sitting on. Julio had given explicit instructions via radio for the past four days. Following close to the plan, he next visited the town's barber for a trim. He would pass to him the precise time and place to gather for the march on the capitol, before moving on to do likewise at the next town's barber shop. Julio sat in the barber chair, like it was just another Tuesday morning. The barber went for his razor and scissors. Julio coolly surveyed the shop.

"8:40. Back of Miguel's Cafe," Julio quietly muttered.

"Huh, what's that?" the seemingly confused barber asked.

Caught off guard, Julio now surmised that the man by the door waiting for a shave must be a spy.

"I see. That's good. Play like you don't hear me."

"What?"

"I'll be sure you get the Red Star for Bravery for your quick thinking, comrade." Julio gave the barber an assuring smile and coyly glanced out into the street.

"That's it." The barber finished.

"Thanks."

Julio winked at the barber and casually departed. He arranged to speed off to the neighboring town. "In the name of the revolution" he was able to borrow a man's horse for a nominal fee. Julio reached the next town and calmly strolled to the barber shop. There, the revolution met its first obstacle. Tacked to the shop's door was a note. The barber had stepped out. He'd be back shortly.

Julio understood all too well the meaning behind the barber's desperate words, scribbled in haste. He had been kidnapped by counter-revolutionaries to thwart the insurrection. Julio rode madly through the town streets, calling out to reassure the townspeople.

"They've taken our barber, but the revolution cannot fail! You there, don't hang your head! They've taken our barber, but the revolution cannot fail!"

His gallant act earned Julio the affectionate nickname "the a-little-off-the-top bandit" for his confusing attention to grooming in the face of a brewing revolution.

The third town proved especially hungry for revolution. Julio rode into the central square about 8 am. Things felt unusually quiet. The calm mood gave the town an eerie sense of anticipation. It was clear by the looks of things that Julio had ridden into a virtual red cell—a people in complete unity with the worker's struggle. Julio trotted lazily through the still streets, tipping his hat politely with a knowing nod to those few whom he passed. He approached the barber's shop and dismounted.

Inside, the barber sat alone reading a newspaper. How convenient, thought Julio, confident that the barber had let it be known that on this morning he was to have a very special customer and, hence, there'd be no wait.

"How's it going?" Julio began.

"Going fine. Fine day it is," the barber, in an all-too-friendly a mood replied, betraying his tense nerves to Julio.

"Don't be nervous, you're doing just fine," Julio voiced under his breath.

"Huh?" The barber gave a spot-on impression of confusion, apparently sensing the room might be bugged. "Just a trim today?"

Catching on, Julio quickly replied, purposely raising his voice. "That's right. Just A Trim! That is the only reason I came into this barber shop. To get a trim and then to leave. I came for no other reason!"

The barber stood behind Julio's chair with a comb and scissors. "Well, ahh, okay then. Let's go for a trim."

"You know why I'll need this trim don't you!?!" Julio asked the barber, continuing to half shout his words.

"Should I?"

"No, certainly not. Absolutely no reason why you, a local barber in a nice, quiet, politically isolated town should have any idea why I, an out-of-town stranger—without care or worry—should need this trim!"

The barber continued his barbering.

Arthur: An Actuarial Odyssey

"You see, I have this 1:15 appointment. An appointment which *you*, a simple barber, would know nothing about."

"I suppose not."

"So you'll be able to remember that, right?"

"Remember what?"

"You know, that I needed this trim for my 1:15 appointment."

"I suppose."

"Well, that's fine. Are you about done with my *trim*— which is the only reason I came into this barber shop?"

"Yep, I think that'll do it."

Julio stood to pay the barber. He casually looked around the barber shop and winked to the barber, before disappearing on horseback on route to the next town.

Over the next few hours Julio rode with a fury from town to town, passing along his revolutionary message. By eleven, Julio had passed the word to all the barbers in all the towns. It was time to commence the next revolutionary steps in the plan. By this point, Arthur had reached the mouth of the north bay. He stood atop the boat's deck and studied the cityscape with his binoculars for any sign of revolutionary fervor. The atmosphere seemed tense, mighty tense—as if a great wave was about to hit the shore and wash across the capitol, thought Arthur.

Arthur: An Actuarial Odyssey

Meanwhile, Julio rode with a cocky, impeccably well-groomed confidence, stopping just outside the capitol, where the converging armies of workers were to meet for their final assault on the forces of reactionary plunder and avarice.

Several hours passed. Julio was initially flustered when the teeming mass of revolutionary workers failed to assemble. Confident that any delay must surely be tactical, Julio took aside a young, revolutionary cadre in his midst. He instructed the young man to loyally wait for the workers' arrival and pass along the order to move on the capitol from the south at precisely 1:15. Julio then made himself a shadow, without form—while remaining gazelle-like—and moved undetectedly throughout the city to scout ahead and create a strategic diversion just before the hour of the assault, adeptly drawing the authority's attention from the advancing plebian army.

Julio rode a city bus to the financial district and stepped off in front of the Monroe Building—the tallest structure on island. Still not having drawn the slightest attention with his uncanny knack for obscurity, he moved half chameleon-like (and half-gazelle-like) to the elevator. The plan was for Julio to work his way to the roof. Again, not wanting to cause any suspicion, he got off on the 33rd floor and took the stairs the final 16 flights; the better not to compromise the mission. Julio and Arthur knew that catching the authorities unaware remained key to victory.

Arthur: An Actuarial Odyssey

As he rounded the stairwell to the 44th floor, the entire worker's movement nearly ground to a halt. A security guard had stooped to tie an *allegedly* untied shoe. Only Julio's calm resolve saved the revolution from its potentially crushing, premature discovery. Relying on a rock solid alibi that he and Arthur concocted for just such an occasion, Julio informed the guard—now peering up at him—that he was a tow truck driver in training. He had always dreamed of representing his people in the Olympics and so remained in a constant state of training readiness, perchance the Olympic Committee should one day answer his letters and grant his petition to make "tow truck hook-up" an official Olympic event.

The guard stood, offering only a circumspect gaze. Julio steadied himself. He was not about to allow a chance encounter to undo all the planning and radio shows that had led up to this moment. He whipped out a wallet photo of himself in an Olympic jump suit waiving the national flag beside a tow truck with a car hooked up and an unidentified man rushing over with a stop watch to congratulate him. The guard was impressed and his national pride got the better of him. He pledged five dollars to Julio's Olympic dream and shouted, "On to Victory!" Julio returned the guard's "On to Victory!" refrain, pocketed the money, and charged up the next flight of stairs.

At last he reached the rooftop. The time was 1:05. There, behind the HVAC unit—just as Arthur and Julio had instructed—Alejandro had secretly stowed a fully equipped hang glider with three stacks of revolutionary leaflets. The plan required Julio to wait until precisely 1:15 and—as the workers' army attacked from the south—he would circle the capitol in the hang glider, dropping hundreds of leaflets to reassure the citizenry. He would then land his glider in the center of the municipal plaza just outside the legislative building where the workers would converge and take over the Halls of Injustice.

Julio waited for the exact moment perched on the roof's edge, grasping handfuls of leaflets and steadying the hang glider. Out in the distant bay he saw the outline of Arthur's boat. Arthur watched the winged figure of Julio through his binoculars and searched the city below for signs of movement. As yet, he saw none. This was a true testament to the discipline of the revolutionary workers, thought Arthur, knowing not even to flinch until the exact hour struck.

Julio looked to the city below and then back to Arthur's waiting ship. The time was 1:14. Then, tragedy. Caught up in revolutionary fervor, Julio gave Arthur a last-second thumbs up and a wave. The motion threw him off balance. He tried to re-gain his footing but the wind caught his glider's wing and hoisted him high into the air out over the city streets. Julio had inadvertently started the revolution ahead of schedule. Arthur looked on aghast from the boat's deck.

Julio was circling the city dropping his revolutionary leaflets but the workers had yet to attack from the south.

Arthur: An Actuarial Odyssey

Having difficulty controlling the hang glider, Julio sailed directionless over the city tossing out his leaflets. Arthur watched helplessly as the wind took Julio much further east than planned. It was clear that Julio's flight path would not land him in the plaza. Rather, the wind continued to pull him dangerously toward the National Prison.

Before he knew what had happened, Julio found himself setting down inside the prison exercise yard. The inmates looked on, curiously studying his leaflets. Misinterpreting the original context of the leaflet's message, the inmates mistook Julio's revolutionary call to "Rise up and Smash the Fascist Powers of Oppression Who Control You with Their Ball and Chains!" for a prison break. Julio brought his glider to rest in the midst of full-scale prison riot. The inmates rushed up and excitedly asked him to share his plan for the mass prison escape. Arthur looked on in despair.

Certain that the advancing worker's army would be able to reach the prison soon, Julio instructed all the inmates to remain patient and not to let their captivity get to them. Help was on the way. An excited roar went through the bustling exercise yard, as the inmates continued with their rioting. The guards retreated to the watch towers. Julio could sense that his words brought comfort to the blood thirsty throng of rioters. He stood atop an overturned piece of exercise equipment to address the masses. The prison guards looked on.

"Hear me oppressed masses!"

Arthur: An Actuarial Odyssey

The rioters up front motioned for those in the rear to give it a rest.

"Listen and hear my words!"

The inmates ratcheted down their rioting.

"I am but an ordinary man! No different from any of you! So, probably you are asking yourself, 'Why did this guy just fly in like this?' Good question. I bring you word of hope! I bring you word of revolution! I bring you word of freedom!"

Again the prisoners went wild.

"But wait!"

Again the prisoners fell silent.

"At this very hour there is a massive army of workers descending upon the city! These are our liberators!"

A collective "hurrah" surged through the inmates.

"At this hour a boat sits just off the coast. On that boat our leader, Generalissimo, awaits my signal that the capitol has been taken and he may come ashore to lead the people! Now, at this point, probably you are wondering what will be your revolutionary roles!?! You are what our great, revolutionary leader, Generalissimo, has called the 'lumpenproletariat.' You are like an open sore infecting the bourgeoisie's bloodstream… a cancer eating away at their intestines… a hideous tumor rotting out their brains—"

Arthur: An Actuarial Odyssey

The inmates seemed to be getting the idea. Julio knew the inmates needed the proper motivation to fulfill their roles.

"The point is this. Your simple role is to cause maximum havoc. You have no place within the bourgeois order. You are the expendable dregs of society. Come the revolution, you've got nothing to lose. All your lives you've known nothing but oppressive poverty and exploitation. So all your pent-up frustrations, your broken dreams—it all comes boiling to the surface and all you can think of is how to cause the greatest amount of mayhem and destruction. So this riot thing we have going here, I like it. I meaning you're giving me really good energy. I feel a lot of raw emotions. But let's, you know, save some of it for the actual destruction of the capitol. Remember, you're all desperate, hopeless men—so let's stay focused. Any questions?"

Several hands shot up.

"You there!"

"As rioters, do you have any suggestions how we can, on the one hand, be called upon to wreak maximum mayhem and destruction while, at the same time, remaining focused on a particular class enemy?"

"Very good question. Did everyone hear that in the back?"

Shouts from the rear asked those up front to raise their voices.

Arthur: An Actuarial Odyssey

"Alright, let me repeat the question. The question was how to both maintain a focus on a particular class enemy while seeking to cause maximum mayhem and destruction? Let's talk for a second about this idea of 'mayhem and destruction.' Can somebody give me a good example of a crazed act of mayhem?"

Again a few hands went up.

"You there!"

"Maybe, for example, when you go to a crowded grocery store with an automatic rifle and shoot out the ceiling, as customers scramble for cover."

There was some disagreement whether the example didn't stray too much into "destruction" as opposed to simple "mayhem," but it was generally agreed that the basic scenario would, indeed, cause mass panic and large-scale confusion—hence, fulfilling the objective of mayhem, properly understood.

"So indeed," Julio continued, "we can go with that example. All I am saying we need to add is to be sure to choose a grocery store in the bourgeois section of town—you see? And the same, of course, goes for wanton acts of destruction. Let's say, you are out of control or striking out madly—that's all very well and good. Just so long as you first choose a distinctly bourgeois target. I think we have time for one more question."

More hands shot up.

Arthur: An Actuarial Odyssey

"I'll take you near the front and then, those who want to, can break up into smaller discussion groups, while others can continue with your rioting to stay fresh—but go easy on the heavy lifting and heaving. Yes, you near the front."

"As I understand it, we are desperately poor men with no real interest in what you call bourgeois society."

"That's right."

"That being the case, how do we stand in relation to those who are poor and exploited, like us, but have been able to find occasional employment to keep them out of prison?"

"Another very good question! For those in the back, I repeat, the question was: How are all of you—as complete outsiders in bourgeois society—supposed to relate to others who are poor but have been able to find jobs in bourgeois society in the context of this whole revolutionary thing we have going here? This is a key point, because, as members of a discarded and forgotten mass of human refuge—"

"Hey!" The crowd grew surly.

"—*in the eyes of bourgeois society that is!*—there's a certain stigma attached to the category of 'prisoner.' Tragically, this is so even in the minds of other exploited workers. This is where the critical role of education comes in. Or, as we in the movement prefer to call it, '*re-education.*' Well, I see that, unfortunately, I have no time

Arthur: An Actuarial Odyssey

to go into further details just right now. However, you can be sure that all such divisions and cleavages within the working-class, as have been sown by the bourgeoisie, will be addressed by our revolutionary leadership!"

The inmates let out wild cheers, as Julio came to a close.

"Now, we must go and negotiate your release with the prison authorities. And rest assured, with the worker's army behind you—by now having surely stormed the capitol—the prison screws will be more than willing to talk."

Triumphant cheers and laughter echoed across the prison yard and the inmates shouted their feral support for the worker's revolution.

Meanwhile, back on his boat, Arthur looked on confused and bewildered. There was still no sign of revolutionary ferment—no workers storming the capitol, no mass hysteria, no actual out-of-the-ordinary activity of any sort. The last he had seen of Julio was the faint outline of his hang glider as he sailed over the prison walls. There was no telling what unspeakable savageries had awaited him inside the confines of that human hell hole. Be that as it may, Arthur stood confident upon the deck that there could be no torture horrible enough, no deprivation cruel enough, no condition of squalor nightmarish enough to break Julio. A lesser man perhaps, but not this trained soldier in the worker's revolutionary movement.

Arthur: An Actuarial Odyssey

Still unaware of the tepid affairs outside the prison walls, Julio arranged to meet with the warden and his men to secure their unconditional surrender of the facility to the inmates. The meeting took place in a conference room around a long, wooden table. Julio, with his lead pipe-wielding lieutenants at his side, pounded the table and demanded that he be issued his own set of keys immediately. The prison officials stared contemptuously.

"Or what?" one of them growled.

Julio sneered. "'Or what?' you ask. 'Or what?' you ask."

Julio grabbed his upper lip, twisted his sneer into a smile, and looked to his two comrades.

"Did you hear him? 'Or what?' he asked."

It was clear that, as Arthur's well-schooled disciple, Julio had inherited much of his master's revolutionary zeal and unrivaled self-confidence. His two lieutenants returned Julio's gawkish smile with a stony, business-like glare. Julio stood and walked over to a radio sitting on a back counter.

"Well, gentlemen, let's just say, Or—this!"

Julio dramatically flipped on the radio, expecting to hear frantic accounts of house-to-house fighting, as the workers took the capitol block by block. Instead, much to Julio's shock, the radio was tuned to a 1970's, easy-listening station which filled the room with Dinah Shore singing "My Way."

Arthur: An Actuarial Odyssey

"Wait a minute!"

Julio ran the dial, searching for news of the armed revolution just beyond the prison gates. He found none. Julio changed tactics.

"I think the important point to bear in mind here is—LOOK!"

Julio pointed out a window and made a dash for the door. Two guards grabbed him and threw him back in his seat.

"Enough of your tricks. Now we know you're the mastermind of the attempted prison break. We just want to know who called for it. What are your connections? Drug lords? The mob? Just how well connected is this outfit that sent you? Who's bankrolling this operation?"

Julio ripped into them. "What are you all thinking? You think this is some petty, turf battle?"

"Just tell us who sent you!"

"I'll tell you who sent me! I'll tell you who sent me! It was the mechanic who quiets the muffler on your car, the maid who cleans your toilets, the nameless face who shines your shoes! I have been sent by a revolutionary class of workers, who I have come to liberate from your bourgeois master's clutches!"

The prison authorities sensed that their initial premonitions about Julio may have been misplaced. Their impression of Julio now suggested less a mastermind from an international, crime ring sent to free mob bosses

Arthur: An Actuarial Odyssey

and more a tragically misled servant of some twisted and dastardly, charismatic leader. Julio's lead pipe-wielding lieutenants soon also had their doubts and asked permission to return to their cells. Julio now sat alone in the conference room with the prison authorities.

"So you're here to liberate the workers?" one of them mused.

Knowing the very thought of this sent shivers down their backs, Julio answered, "Until the last drop of bourgeois blood is spilt."

"Oooh, tough guy? You know what I think, I think—"

Suddenly a guard rushed into the conference room and handed off a note to the warden who scanned it quickly and turned to speak to a few other prison officials. There was initial confusion. Julio sat quietly, confident that the note brought good news from the front lines of the worker's battles in the capitol.

"Okay," the official holding the note told the guard. "Bring him in."

Julio turned to face the door. The guard ushered in an older man, slight in build. Julio thought he recognized him from somewhere. It was one of the barbers! Julio was horrified. They'd captured one of the movement's barbers! Untrained to withstand the cruel torture tactics of the bourgeoisie, Julio knew he would crack in seconds.

Arthur: An Actuarial Odyssey

"Yeah, that's the guy," the barber blurted out, clearly having been worked over in some hideous back room. "That's the nut who came by my barber shop acting all weird about 'worker's struggle' and stuff."

"Alright, that's enough. Get him out of here," the junta stooge snorted.

As they led the barber out, Julio lashed out at the guards. "You animals! What barbarism have you dreamed up to force this man to talk!?!" Then to reassure the barber, he added, "Don't worry soldier. Your place in the history of worker's struggle is secure! Your unspeakable torture will be a testament to every worker's sacrifice!"

The warden leaned in and whispered to one of the guards. The other prison officials rose and left the room. A guard motioned for Julio to follow him out.

"You don't scare me! You robotic fascist!"

Julio followed the guard from the room.

"Go ahead. Take your best shot. Drag me to some remote dungeon and spare no torture!"

The guard continued, with Julio following behind.

"You got thumbscrews? Well, I eat thumbscrews for breakfast, buddy. You got a rack? Well I take my naps on a rack—you dirty screw!"

The guard led Julio down a long, dim, and cluttered corridor. The two came to a door and the guard told Julio to wait there while he went inside. Julio stood in the dark hallway. He thought about running but he knew that was exactly what they wanted—so he could take one in the back. The guard returned with a large set of keys.

"Hah! You thought I'd take off. You thought you could drop me with a rifle shot. Well think again."

The guard continued down the corridor, studying his wad of keys.

"Oh, so that's it," Julio continued. "You've got your little torture chamber tucked away somewhere down this forgotten passageway. Well hurry up and find the key, I haven't eaten for a while. I want to taste that first electric volt!"

The guard found his key and appeared to have reached the right room. He opened the door, as Julio continued his taunts. The guard told Julio to step inside.

"Gladly," Julio boasted.

The guard slammed the door behind him and Julio stood momentarily blinded by a brilliant shaft of light that flooded the room. The heat from the light nearly burnt his skin. This was a torture unknown to Julio. Slowly, he became better oriented. He saw now that the dazzling light was actually the sun. Incredible as it seemed, the guard had apparently opened the wrong door, leaving him outside the prison walls. Julio stood looking up at the prison gates from the street, amused by the buffoonery of his captors.

Arthur: An Actuarial Odyssey

Anxious to avoid re-capture, a rejuvenated Julio hurried through the streets in search of the worker's army to re-join the battle. Slowly it dawned on Julio that the worker's revolution may not be proceeding precisely on schedule. In fact, by all outward appearances, one could conclude that the revolutionary call to action had gone completely unheeded. Julio nervously continued along the city streets, alternating now between fears of re-capture and fears of a mugging. He reached the road just outside the capitol where all the workers planned to meet. There was no sign of anyone.

Dismayed and disillusioned, Julio returned to the rooftop of the Monroe Building and dejectedly gave Arthur the signal to abort the mission. The uprising had failed. Arthur, observing the workers' movement fizzle from the boat, sadly acknowledged Julio's signal. Arthur had completely misread the worker's consciousness. Somehow he had mistaken chastened chagrin and genuine apathy for a spirited insurrectionist zeal. Julio was most disappointed of all. Inconsolable, a few days after the failed uprising, he returned to baggage handling at the airport, a soldier lost to the revolutionary movement forever.

Arthur decided to move on. It was time, he thought, to get on with his life and resume his desperate search for meaning and purpose. The next day he boarded a plane and headed back home from whence his journey had begun. He caught sight of Julio down below loading the baggage, and pounded his fist on the window pane. But

Arthur: An Actuarial Odyssey

wearing his protective ear plugs, Julio was oblivious to the hysterically gesturing Arthur only 30 feet away.

Arthur fastened his seat belt, returned his seat to its locked, up-right position and was off. After so many weeks secluded in the mountains, the airline food seemed a true delicacy to Arthur. He passed on his compliments to the chef through a flight attendant who, to quell Arthur's incessant requests, put a note on the microwave.

Arthur: An Actuarial Odyssey

Chapter Seventeen

Arthur was, by nature, a nervous flyer. He removed the seat cushion from the middle seat to examine it as a flotation device. He tossed it up in the air but it just fell back down into his lap. He tried again and again. But again and again, it just fell back into his lap. In a panic, he buzzed for the flight attendant and explained that his flotation device would not float. And he held it up and dropped into his lap to demonstrate. The flight attendant snatched the cushion out of the air and put it back in the middle seat. Arthur was comforted only slightly to learn that it was not designed to float in the air—only in water. He asked the flight attendant to please bring him 55 cups of water. Again, she re-assured Arthur that all seat cushions were thoroughly tested before putting them on the plane.

Arthur tried to relax. He spotted two men a few rows ahead wearing headphones. The flight attendant told Arthur he could have a pair for four dollars. Arthur thought four dollars was a bit much for a piece of airplane

Arthur: An Actuarial Odyssey

technology that looked as if it had not been updated since the Zeppelin flew. Besides, he didn't even know what those guys were listening to. Perhaps, Arthur thought, the airline hired these guys to take flights and wear the headphones pretending to be having a really jolly time. That way, everyone will see them and think, hey, those guys are having a really jolly time, maybe I should pay four dollars to get a pair of headphones too.

But maybe in reality they're just listening to stock market reports. Or maybe they *are* just other passengers but they happen to be huge Tony Orlando and Dawn fans. By the time the plane lands they'll have the whole cabin swaying back and forth singing about "tying a yellow ribbon round an old oak tree." The flight attendant was losing patience. Finally, Arthur decided to go ahead with the headphones.

Unfortunately, Arthur's timing could not have been worse. The flight attendants had just passed through the cabin with their complimentary beverage service. Arthur declined the liquids they offered. However, the man behind Arthur grabbed a coffee. Arthur connected his headphones, pulled them snug to his ears, and leaned back in his seat to relax. He then dialed in his headset just in time to hear the bloodcurdling scream from the man behind him. Arthur ripped off his headphones, sat straight up, and sternly summoned the flight attendant.

He asked just what kind of twisted airlines were they running that made people pay four dollars to hear horrific screams of agony when they were just trying to relax. He

Arthur: An Actuarial Odyssey

had her take a listen, but everything seemed fine. Accepting this to have been a peculiar, inexplicable mishap, Arthur took back the headphones. Once more, he put them on, leaned back—again splashing coffee all over the man behind him—and the bloodcurdling screams returned. Arthur was incensed. He called the flight attendant back over.

She suggested he try another channel—perhaps easy listening. By this point the man seated behind Arthur had left for the lavatory to clean himself up. Arthur put the headphones on and, indeed, now found a suitable station. Still, Arthur was quite upset and he told the flight attendant that he could not understand why the airline would insist on a radio format of classical music, easy listening, stock reports, and tortured screams of agony.

Arthur decided to just kick back and relax with the in-flight movie. Again, however, in his anxious state, Arthur felt in need of clarification. He called the flight attendant to ask why they airline called it an "in-flight" movie. Why not just call it a movie? Were they suggesting that if there were engine trouble and the plane rolled into a nosedive that they would suddenly switch to the "while-crashing" movie? He didn't recall seeing theaters advertise their "while-sitting-in-a-building" movies.

The flight attendant explained that this was simply industry jargon for watching a movie on a plane—nothing more. Arthur was skeptical but sat back and joined the other passengers to enjoy the six-hour, director's cut of

Arthur: An Actuarial Odyssey

"Apocalypse Now." Soon, however, initially finding the action a bit slow, Arthur peacefully drifted off to sleep.

Then, almost halfway into the thriller, there were some technical problems. A collective sigh carried through the cabin as the screen went dark. The audio was fine but the crew worked to restore the picture. A flight attendant explained that it should just take a few minutes to fix. Meanwhile, they ran the airline safety video. Soon, however, there were audio problems as well. As a result, the feature film's sound track was playing over the airline's safety video. There were a few chuckles and then passengers removed their headsets or switched to another channel temporarily. Arthur, however, deep in slumber, awoke horrified to see a smiling flight attendant holding out an oxygen mask and screaming, "Die you dirty bastard! DIE!"

After brought up to speed, Arthur re-read his laminated emergency landing instruction sheet to help settle his nerves. He called one of the flight attendants over to identify the model of the plane they were on and she pointed it out on his sheet. He asked if she had ever actually had to use the exit slide to escape from burning wreckage. She said that she had only done so in training. Arthur again panicked. In training!?! If they hadn't even been able to make a practice run of a plane flight without ending up barely escaping from a twisted, ball of flames, what chance did they have now of every reaching the ground alive? The excitement of Arthur's worried tone started a mild panic among the surrounding passengers.

Arthur: An Actuarial Odyssey

The flight attendant calmly re-assured passengers, via the cabin intercom, that the plane was not about to fall from the sky. As she concluded her remarks about the airline's safety record, Arthur stood and grabbed the mike from her to add some remarks.

"People, now at such a harrowing hour, I think it is crucial that we maintain complete confidence in the cabin crew."

The flight attendant tried to grab back the mike.

"They have been nothing less than professional, attentive, and courteous. Nonetheless, there are certain topics which professional etiquette obviously prevents them from fully sharing. Does anyone here suffer from any kind of heart problems?"

A hush went through the cabin. Several persons called out that they, indeed, had some heart issues.

"Now, now, it's nothing to worry about. However, were we to crash and burn on impact, the procedures for exiting the plane may take its toll on a few of you. Now, how many of you have plummeted, let's say, 40 feet on a piece of foam rubber onto a hard, concrete surface, as our flight attendant was forced to do when a routine training flight went tragically wrong?"

The flight attendant pulled the mike away from Arthur and instructed him to take his seat. She reiterated that everything was proceeding with nothing, whatsoever, out of the ordinary and that everyone should simply sit back

Arthur: An Actuarial Odyssey

and enjoy the flight. Arthur took his seat and tried to relax with a copy of the airline's in-flight magazine, *Up, Up and Away*. He was nearly half-way through a fascinating inside look at "Trout Fishing with Ben Vereen in the Himalayas" when a disturbing full-page ad nearly sent him back over the edge. It featured a picture of some airline captain smiling to the camera with a caption reading, "Hi, I'm Captain Stevenson, and I'm an alcoholic." Fortunately, Arthur recalled that the captain for this flight was a Captain Richardson.

This was turning into quite a long flight, Arthur thought. He sat staring out the window at the endless blue sky. To entertain himself, he imagined that the clouds formed little animals. In the innocence of one's imagination there are no limits to a wondrous world of gaiety and simple pleasures. There was a giraffe leaping over a goat, a tiger tossing a beach ball to a zebra, a bull dancing with an elephant, a young, angelic boy in a flowing white robe warning those in the plane to go back, go back, do not cross over to the wicked side. Arthur quickly shut his window shade and put his headphones back on. In his nervous state his mind was simply playing tricks on him. Some soothing, classical music should help restore his serenity and peace.

The plane hit some slight turbulence and Arthur cranked up the Mozart. The ride was bumpy but the violins kept Arthur calm. He could feel the music surrounding him. The soaring strings, supported by the soulful brass and all made whole by the woodwinds

Arthur: An Actuarial Odyssey

brought an airy relief to Arthur's unease. He sat back and let the soothing music glide over him. In mid-interlude, the captain briefly spoke to reassure passengers about the minor turbulence.

"Sorry for the interruption folks. This is Capt—"

Suddenly the mike went dead. Another voice then spoke from the cockpit.

"No need to panic there folks. This is your co-pilot, Captain Stevenson—hiccup. Captain Richardson is feeling a bit under the weather—hiccup—but don't worry. These birds are made for only one person to handle them anyway—hiccup. Whoops, I seem to have a slight case of the hiccups. At any rate—hiccup—we just wanted to let you know that we're having some slight turbulence—hiccup. But we should be through it in 10 minutes or so. So you all should just—hiccup—sit back and enjoy the rest of the flight."

Arthur flew into a state of complete panic. Captain Richardson had passed out and now the entire crew and passengers were under the command of the poster boy for Alcoholics Anonymous. The most important thing, thought Arthur, was not to cause a panic among the other passengers. He waited for the turbulence to pass and the fasten-seat-belt light to dim. Then, very nonchalantly, Arthur made his way through the cabin like he was just heading for the bathroom. At the last second he snatched the microphone for the cabin's intercom.

Arthur: An Actuarial Odyssey

"May I have your attention! May I have your attention! Do not panic! Repeat, do not panic! At this time, we need to know whether there are any professionally trained alcohol and drug abuse counselors on board!?! Repeat, are there any professionally trained alcohol and drug abuse counselors on board!?! We may need your services to land this plane. Please make yourselves known to a flight attendant whenever—"

A flight attendant rushed up, grabbed the mike, and returned Arthur to his seat. For the rest of the flight, Arthur sat with his arms glued to the armrests. He repeatedly ran through the details of the emergency exit procedures in his mind. As Captain Stevenson announced the final approach for landing, Arthur readied himself. He had put his seat in the upright position for the past two hours. He closed the window shade to protect from flying glass. He drew his seat belt tight to his midsection, removed all loose items from around his seat, shouted "we're going down!" and tucked his head beneath his legs while clasping the back of his head with his hands.

Moments later, as the plane taxied to its gate, Arthur finally raised his head, expecting to find bodies strewn about the cabin and passengers writhing in agony. Miraculously, the landing had gone without a hitch. Arthur thanked the flight crew and raced for the terminal.

The plane ride home had been a sobering, soul-searching experience and only served to re-double Arthur's commitment to find the meaning and purpose of life as soon as possible. There were secrets to this wacky

Arthur: An Actuarial Odyssey

universe still beyond his grasp, as Arthur explained to the cab driver, and he didn't want to waste another moment waiting to resume his quest. The cab driver seemed impressed, Arthur felt. The cabby asked where he wanted to begin his searching. Arthur smiled.

"You know, all my life I've planned out exactly what to do, where to go, what to say, how to act, what to wear, who to see, where to stay—"

"I get the idea mac, but I gotta take the cab somewhere."

"I tell you what. I don't know about you, but I'm sick of these narrow, social conventions, these suffocating and arbitrary titles and distinctions—cab driver, passenger. I've just survived a harrowing, near-tragic plane ride. To hell with tradition. Let's live on the edge. Why must the passenger always decide where to go? This time, you decide. Tell me nothing. Simply nod when we have arrived and I shall exit. No one but you and I will ever know that it was you, the cab driver, and not I, the passenger, who decided our destiny."

"Whatever," the driver mumbled as he started off.

"Tell me, how does it feel to have complete control over another man's destiny? Total command of another's fate?"

"Hey, it's all I can do not to wet myself, know what I mean?"

Arthur smiled.

Arthur: An Actuarial Odyssey

"I must tell you, I find such mockery quite refreshing. Everyone always feels they must be so polite, so controlled. But you—though you hardly know me at all—feel as if you can insult me to my face, openly degrade me with smug, sarcastic remarks. I feel myself liberated by your bold indiscretion."

"Yeah, my friends often tell me to work on my self-assertiveness problem."

"Delightful, absolutely delightful. You act as if completely free of any social customs whatsoever. You must tell me, what is your secret? How have you broken from those social rules of etiquette asking us to offer up an arsenal of polite facades and disingenuous niceties?"

"Well, I guess part of it comes from having so little to live for."

"You don't say."

Arthur noticed the cab seemed to be speeding up.

"Well, when your wife leaves you and you lose your job to some hot-shot advertising kid…"

The cab was now hurtling through traffic.

"Sounds rough."

"…so you end up drivin' pretentious assholes around in a stinkin' cab to make ends meet. And the hours just get longer, the driving endless."

The cab wove unpredictably at a breakneck speed, as terrified pedestrians dove from its path.

Arthur: An Actuarial Odyssey

Arthur clutched the back of the front seat, his limbs frozen.

"Hey, how about that NAFTA? Bummer, eh?"

"It's to the point where everywhere I turn all I can see is that freakin' lawyer's face. And all I want to do is—SMASH IT!"

The cab barreled along nearly out-of-control.

"I tell you what, let's re-think that slightly generalized critique of social etiquette for a sec'."

Suddenly the cab leaped the center highway barrier. The two were rocketing along the wrong side of the road, forcing on-coming traffic to veer off the road.

Arthur tried desperately to re-contextualize his previous thoughts.

"I think Mencius said it best when—"

"My whole life lies in ruins. The doctors… they all say take it easy… get some rest. Be careful, they say, before something sends me over the edge. Well, Do I Look Over The Edge!?! DO I LOOK OVER THE EDGE!?!"

"Not a chance. Take it from me, I've seen over the edge and this, heck, this isn't close. What say we grab ourselves a coffee and talk this out?"

The horns and sirens drowned out most of Arthur's words.

Arthur: An Actuarial Odyssey

"You know the funny part," the cabbie continued.

"The funny part? What would that be?"

The world outside rushed past Arthur's window in a naked blur.

"After all these years—"

Arthur felt the cold stare of death upon his face.

"—all these years of wondering, where did I go wrong, what did I do to deserve this? And it turns out it was just because I was a nice guy. Nice guys really do finish last. Well… it's NO MORE MR. NICE GUY!!!"

These were the last words Arthur heard before his cab tumbled down an embankment, rolled several times, and exploded into a massive fire ball. Arthur's ragged body was thrown from the twisted wreckage and lay lifeless a few yards from the inferno. Arthur felt very peculiar. At first he could not feel anything. Then a prickly sensation completely paralyzed his left, pinky toe. Everything grew dark and the rest of his senses were numbed. Suddenly, his toe felt fine and there was a brilliant white light shining ahead of him. The light sat at the end of a long, dark tunnel. A rush of emotions swept over Arthur. It was as if someone—or something—was calling Arthur to move forward. To go into the light.

A peaceful serenity embraced Arthur as he felt himself pulled more and more into the bright white orb just ahead of him. A blanket of warmth engulfed him. From out of nowhere, a collection of Arthur's deceased relatives

Arthur: An Actuarial Odyssey

suddenly appeared. Each took on a cloudy, mystical form and stretched their arms, reaching out to Arthur. Thinking at first that they may want money, Arthur pulled back and their images dissipated. The light grew ever brighter and Arthur could now hear a muffled voice calling out to him.

"Arthur, Arthur."

"Who's there!?!" Arthur cried.

"Arthur, Arthur."

"Who is it? I can't see with all the light."

"Arthur, Arthur."

"Enough with the 'Arthur, Arthur'—who the hell is there?"

"It is I."

"Well… yes. But technically speaking, I am also I. Which I is you?"

"It is I the Giver of Life, the Source of all Knowledge, the One who Judges all Others."

Arthur knew that voice. He grew excited.

"Uncle Herbie!"

Arthur's long lost Uncle Herbie appeared before him.

"Still, the practical joker here in the after-life, eh, Uncle Herbie?"

"How'd you know it was me?" Uncle Herbie coyly replied.

Arthur: An Actuarial Odyssey

"That's how you used to always answer the phone. So what the hell's going on? I can't really be dead, can I?"

"What's the last thing you remember before ending up here?"

"Careening off the highway and crashing in a burning inferno."

"Well, I'm no doctor, but—"

"I can't believe it! I mean... So what's the deal? Is there somewhere to check-in or something?"

"Someone will come for you."

"How will I recognize them?"

"They will give you a sign."

"A sign? What kind of a sign?"

"They'll say something like, 'I've come for you.'"

"I guess I'll just wait then. So where is everybody?"

"Who?"

"Well, you know other dead relatives—or maybe some famous dead people. Hey, that'd be something. You seen Socrates? Where's Lincoln? What about Hendrix!?!"

"Surprisingly enough, you don't really see a lot of celebrities."

"I guess they've got their own special, VIP section," Arthur surmised.

Arthur: An Actuarial Odyssey

"No, here in the ever-after we are all in the same trailer park."

"Trailer park!?! You mean the after-life is spent for all eternity living in a trailer park!?!" Arthur was indignant.

"Well, you see, you've got to be philosophical about it. For most people here, a trailer park is quite a step up. Remember, a large number of the folks here lived their lives as simple hunter-gatherers. When I first got here, I had neighbors on one side of me—nicest people you'd ever want to meet—but a very limited vocabulary. They mostly grunted and made faces. To be honest, they were quite primitive when I first met them. But now, you should see the difference. They put on the best barbecues. Even my neighbor on the other side—an admittedly anti-social, late 18th-Century Dutch banker and his family—have joined in lately."

"I can't believe it." Arthur sulked. "Stuck for all eternity in a trailer park with Neolithic Man." Changing the subject, Arthur asked, "So have you met Him?"

"Him?"

"You know—Him. The Big Cheese. God Almighty."

"Oh right, Him. Bad news. Turns out. No God."

"What? No God? So, who runs the place?"

"There's some controversy over that. By the time I got here people had just stopped asking."

"So this is death."

Arthur: An Actuarial Odyssey

"This is it. You gotta admit that light thing they do when people first arrive is pretty nifty."

"Yeah, what was the deal with that?"

"It's supposed to help people find their way. Before they came up with the brilliant, white light effect, they had a large sound truck that went around with a recorded message saying, 'Psssst, buddy, over hear.' People got to thinkin' it was too impersonal. So we came up with the light thing."

"But wouldn't anyone just eventually find their way?"

"Maybe. The main thing is to stop folks from going over to the competition."

"You mean there's more than one after-life?"

"Sure."

"So the whole light show is just a marketing ploy?"

"By and large. Here, I guess you didn't get our brochure."

Uncle Herbie handed Arthur a brochure for the Permanent Rest Stop and Trailer Park.

"But I don't get it. What are the other after-life places like? What are the options?"

Suddenly a bolt of lightning lit up the sky and thunder echoed across the horizon. Uncle Herbie's image faded before disappearing into a foggy mist. Arthur stood alone in a large field. There were mountains well off in the distance. Otherwise, the field's rolling expanse stretched out well beyond what Arthur could see. Far ahead of him, Arthur saw some figure in a flowing, white robe. The figure was approaching from across the field. Arthur started walking toward the figure but his feet plunged through the muddy field's mushy surface. With each step he sank deeper.

Chapter Eighteen

Meanwhile, back at his discarded body, the emergency crew worked furiously to revive Arthur. They were about to measure him for a toe tag when suddenly—a miracle.

"Hey! I think we've got a pulse!" a paramedic called out.

Arthur's body was rushed to Heaven's Gate Hospital where doctors worked around the clock to resuscitate his barely breathing corpse. After 11 hours of surgery his body's vital signs were sputtering and faint, but strengthening.

Arthur sank more deeply into the thick mounds of mud as the white-robed figure moved towards him across the massive field.

Arthur was nearly stabilized and his body was nearing consciousness.

All but his head and neck were now buried beneath the muddy surface.

For a brief flash Arthur's body opened its eyes.

Arthur: An Actuarial Odyssey

Arthur slipped down through the muddy field's grasp and just continued falling.

Arthur's eyes suddenly shut and his body lapsed into a deep coma.

Arthur kept falling, softly breaking through a bedrock of clouds.

The doctors lay Arthur's body in a quiet, recovery room to wait out the coma.

Arthur was falling as if aiming for the hospital. He was angling straight for his body's hospital room. Arthur sensed that he was about to rejoin his body, that a terrible wrong had been righted—that he was not meant to die this day. Arthur rejoiced as he crashed through the hospital roof, breaking through ceilings and floors on route to his body's 9th floor recovery room.

"I'm coming! I'm coming! Hold on body!" Arthur cried out. "I'll be right—"

Arthur blacked out. A few seconds later, he found himself awake and being prepped for childbirth. Still groggy and disoriented, Arthur did not immediately realize that he had just entered his 10th hour of labor.

"Thank God! Thank God that's over! For a while there I thought—Oh my God!" Arthur screamed hysterically.

Arthur had returned from the other side only to re-enter the wrong body. He had mistakenly entered the body of a very young, very Caucasian woman just moments from giving birth. Arthur desperately tried to

Arthur: An Actuarial Odyssey

explain this mix up to others in the room. But no one could hear him or sense his presence in any way. Arthur's out-of-body experience had ended with a completely botched re-entry.

The doctor propped up Arthur with his feet in the stirrups and told him to relax as she spread his legs and began to probe him. Arthur felt things he had never felt before. The nurse wiped the sweat from his brow. The doctor commanded that Arthur push as hard as he could. In vain, Arthur continued to explain the troubling switcheroo and the great risk this posed for HIPAA violations. A distinct, sharp pain shot through Arthur's body as his Caucasian baby struggled to escape.

Arthur was going to experience the miracle of child birth first-hand. The doctor announced that she could see the crown of the baby's head. Arthur took deep, rapid breaths and braced himself for one last, mighty push. The doctor amplified her call.

"Come on sister, that's one last push for motherhood! Show 'em just what kind of a woman you are!"

Arthur gave it one last shove, exhausting the last of his energies. At last, the room filled with a baby's cry. The nurse brought a teary-eyed Arthur his newborn baby.

"And what shall we call your fine, healthy son?"

Arthur tried to speak but the words of the woman whose body he had re-entered drown out his own voice and thoughts.

Arthur: An Actuarial Odyssey

"Arthur," she answered.

Oh, the irony, Arthur thought. He listened as the woman explained why she had chosen the name. There was something familiar—hauntingly familiar—about that voice. Arthur knew he had heard it somewhere before... when he was... a child and—suddenly it hit him like a ton of Freudian tits. That was the voice of his very own Caucasian mother!

Arthur was dumbstruck. Was this possibly connected to his search for the meaning and purpose of life? Were the Gods merely playing some cruel trick on him? That must be it, Arthur thought. He had come too close to discovering the ultimate truths of the universe. The Gods, jealous and spiteful, coveted Arthur's sage-like brilliance. Now, both to punish him and to forever insure that the hidden secrets of the universe would remain a guarded mystery, the Gods had returned Arthur to his infant stage.

Their cruelty knowing no bounds, they would force Arthur to go back and watch himself grow up and live out his life in complete ignorance of those hidden truths. He would watch encased in silence as he himself—through little Arthur—grew into an imbecilic, clueless brute content and happy with his routine and empty existence robbed of any meaning or purpose.

"No, wait a minute," the woman exclaimed. "What am I thinking? Not 'Arthur'—I meant Bubba."

On hearing her voice a second time, Arthur recognized that his fears had been misplaced. This was no mother of

Arthur: An Actuarial Odyssey

his. Greatly relieved, he and little Bubba were wheeled out of the delivery room. The nurses took Bubba to the nursery and Arthur was sent to the recovery wing of the maternity ward. Everyone congratulated Arthur on his beautiful baby boy and told him what a wonderful job he had done dislodging the infant. Fatigue soon came over Arthur and the nurses suggested he get some sleep. They doped him up and Arthur felt deep fatigue before soon falling off to sleep.

Arthur woke hours later to find he had once more abandoned any bodily form and was now hovering in a corner of the young mother's hospital room. He had some difficulty at first maneuvering about as a disembodied spirit. He would push off a wall to move to his left or right but sometimes his immaterial "hand" would pass through the wall and at other times he would bounce uncontrollably about the room. After a few further tries, Arthur got the hang of moving about as a spirit. Now freed to move about the hospital, he set off in search of his body.

Returning from the dead, giving birth, and now existing without bodily form had opened Arthur's eyes to many new things. The scope and wonder of the universe seemed even greater than he had once imagined. Arthur sought only to rejoin his body and resume his search for the meaning and purpose of life, now with a renewed vigor and a broadened perspective. He'd stared death in the face and won. He'd experienced the beauty and

Arthur: An Actuarial Odyssey

majesty of bringing a new life into the world first hand. Now he was floating about, freed of corporeal bondage.

Arthur knew that these were all signs that a power greater than he had chosen *him* to bring some message to all the people of the world. He began to make a mental list of all the afternoon tv talk shows he would go on—knowing he had only to find the Black-male-sexual-deviance angle to his experiences to guarantee an appearance. For now, he had merely to continue exploring what that message could be.

Arthur's immediate challenge was to find his body and somehow re-enter it. Now largely able to command the speed and direction of his disembodied hovering, Arthur managed to lower himself through the doorway and out into the hallway. He knew that his body was somewhere on the seventh floor but he was not yet sure how best to change floors. First he tried the elevator. But he found it impossible to work the buttons. His formless, spiritual finger would simply push through the actual button each time he "pressed" it. Next he tried the stairs. But Arthur found that doors continued to pose problems without bodily form.

Basically, existing as a formless spirit was good for little more than floating about rooms undetected. Though at first intriguing for Arthur, spiritual mobility seemed quite limited. Initially, assuming that as a spiritual being he shouldn't have much difficulty passing through physical objects, Arthur tried to simply "crash" through floors and ceilings on his way to the seventh floor. This

Arthur: An Actuarial Odyssey

proved unworkable. Arthur found it impossible to calibrate the speed and trajectory of his smashing through solid objects and he would consistently over-shoot or under-shoot the seventh floor.

Arthur decided it would be easiest to wait for a person with human form to enter the elevator, follow them in, and simply wait for someone to get off on the seventh floor. Arthur was startled to find two other spiritual forms also waiting by the elevator. He approached the pair but they just hovered in stony silence—apparently unable to sense his presence.

One of the spirits turned to the other and asked, "How many you got today?"

"Just three. You?"

"Same. Any surprises?"

"Not really. Congested heart failure, diabetes, the usual."

"Yeah, same here."

The elevator doors slid open. Two humans stepped out and one human entered. The two spirits followed the human in, with Arthur right behind.

"Any of yours go suddenly?"

"Nah, pretty much all their time to go. Except 714, of course."

Arthur: An Actuarial Odyssey

"Yeah, I heard some of the dispatchers talkin' about that guy. What a lame dweeb. I hear they gave the guy every chance in the world."

"Ain't that the truth. First Bernard screws up the pick-up so they have to send him back. Then they give him all these signs to figure out what's what. But nothing registers. Clueless bozo."

"Try and figure."

The elevator doors opened and another human wandered in.

"Yep. Hey, isn't this your 412?"

"Whoa, almost missed it—thanks. Be seein' ya."

"Right."

Their conversation made Arthur uneasy, though he wasn't sure why. These were clearly not other spirits like him in search of bodies to re-join. These seemed to be spirits in search of bodies to take away, harvester spirits so to speak. They were delivering death notices. Arthur maneuvered to the right of the harvester spirit to glimpse his casualty list. His notepad listed the dead persons, their location, and their cause of death. Arthur read along. The harvester spirit's work order detailed one sad case after another. The list included mostly those in their 70's and 80's suffering from a variety of routine ailments.

Continuing down the list, Arthur felt a cold chill when he came across a young man cut down in the prime of life. The details sounded so familiar, so recognizable.

Arthur: An Actuarial Odyssey

Most peculiar, thought Arthur, was the cause of death—"after much searching, could not find the meaning and purpose of life." In a panic, Arthur raced through the rest of the death notice to find the poor unfortunate's name. Arthur's spiritual form released a disembodied gasp. The harvester spirit's pick-up in room 714 was none other than Arthur himself. Arthur's search for the meaning and purpose of life was now a race against time for his very soul. The harvester spirit had stops on the fifth and sixth floors before reaching his room. If Arthur did not discover the meaning and purpose of life before the spirit reached his body's bedside he knew he was doomed.

Arthur lurked behind the harvester spirit as he wafted along the fifth floor corridor in search of his retrieval. The harvester spirit entered the dying patient's room, an elderly man surrounded by close friends and family. As Arthur trailed the harvester spirit into the room. The patient lapsed in and out of consciousness. The nurse administered narcotics, while a doctor studied his charts. The family minister stood with solemn poise beside the dying patient's children and spouse. The harvester spirit hovered in a nearby corner of the room, checking his notes and filling out some last minute paperwork. Even the inevitable, it seemed, required careful planning meticulous preparation.

Finally, the doctor stepped away from the patient with sober resignation. He consoled the family and confessed he could now help only to ease the pain of dying. The minister stepped in with prayerful recitations. Friends and

Arthur: An Actuarial Odyssey

family wept and bid farewell to the man who lay dying. At last, with the nurse now disengaging the monitors, the harvester spirit made his move. He dove down to greet the dearly departed. The deceased took his demise well. He reviewed his options with the harvester spirit and retreated to an upper corner of the room to fill out forms and plan eternity. The scene below, meanwhile, was filled with tearful sorrow.

It was clear that in death no one—not doctors with all their fancy technology, not nurses with their morphine drips, not ministers with all their elaborate interstellar connections—no one, could bring comfort or lessen the pain and sorrow of those losing someone so dear.

The irony struck Arthur. On one plane, for the living, death arrived as deep tragedy. On a separate plane, for the dying, death promised emancipation. Yes! Arthur thought to himself. Of course! That must be it! This must somehow connect to the meaning and purpose of life. The deepest secrets of the universe, etc., etc. He repeated these thoughts to himself excitedly, waiting for a sign. There was none. Wrong again, Arthur thought. His search must continue. He and the harvester spirit returned to the elevator. The harvester spirit shuffled his work orders, as Arthur spiritually paced nervously back and forth.

A distraught couple stepped off the elevator on the sixth floor. The harvester spirit followed behind, late for his 604 pick-up. He turned down a hallway with Arthur in tow and found room 604 overflowing with activity. Nurses and doctors rushed in and out. Family members

Arthur: An Actuarial Odyssey

crowded doorways and stairwells. Then, as the harvester spirit scribbled some last second thoughts, the clamor and commotion suddenly ceased. A grim-faced doctor pulled the bed sheet over the still patient and withdrew from the bedside.

The nurses gathered their instruments, quieted their monitors, and excused themselves from the scene. The family minister knelt in prayer and found a vacant corner to console the grieving. Arthur looked on, seeing that nothing could stem their sorrow, ease their pain, or bring them solace—not the finest medical doctors and nurses, not the noblest friends and family, not even the Godliest minister. All stood by—feeble, naked, impotent—at this, the darkest hour of human existence that awaits us all.

This then was the moment when, for Arthur, the celestial Heavens opened, the source of supreme and ultimate truth and meaning came into view, and all questions became superfluous, all answers immaterial. As he watched the scene unfold below, a small, undistinguished figure dressed in black and toting a grey attaché case entered and stepped to the middle of the room. Friends and family members—absorbed in their bereavement—parted, creating a phalanx through which the mysterious intruder passed. All eyed him, with both sorrow and curiosity.

The little man waited for a pair of orderlies to remove the expired patient's corpse and he then slapped his attaché case down at the foot of the bed. Before opening the case he shared a business card. This was the dead

Arthur: An Actuarial Odyssey

man's life insurance agent. With that, the small man clad in black cracked open the attaché case full of crisp bills, most featuring Ben Franklin's handsome profile. The dearly departed's dearly departure turned out to be a sizable cash bonanza for the living.

At last! Arthur had his answers. All it required was a slight twist of phrase. We must ask not what the living can do for the dying, but what the dying can do for the living. The dead have their emancipation to comfort them. The living are left only with their sorrow and grief, until… little men with their little black suits and little grey attaché cases appear on the scene. Hence, the meaning and purpose of life was simple: To make the act of dying itself not merely a painful moment of grief and loss but an occasion for money to profitably exchange hands. Death need not result simply in tragic, empty loss.

Death itself could be a source of material gain. Before the advent of life insurance, people just died—their rotted corpses thoughtlessly plowed back into the Earth. Now people no longer simply expired—they could be cashed in. Only life insurance agents could bring meaning and *value* to death—and put an actual dollar figure on it. Indeed, life insurance agents alone possessed the power of true redemption! True recompence!

In fact, Arthur had his answer all along. But deceived by his warped, idyllic sense of human fulfillment he simply would not see. Now all was clear. The life insurance agent did not create meaning and purpose to rectify people's empty, sterile lives. It was people's

Arthur: An Actuarial Odyssey

empty, sterile lives—and their profound lack of meaning and purpose—that created the life insurance agent. To make it rain was his purpose. To bring closure in times of grief with a new 60-inch plasma television was how he helped people find meaning.

Arthur fell back against a curtain rod, rocked by the profundity of his own depth of insight. He could feel—if but fleetingly—the transcendental power of this revelation; as if he, a mere mortal, walked among the Prophets. With sudden celestial force, a lightning bolt ripped through the room, hurling Arthur's disembodied form through the wall. His head spinning, his spiritual form racing along like an electric current, Arthur found himself sucked back into the material world of mortals. His spirit rode atop the lightning bolt until, with an unceremonial thud, Arthur found himself resting on a hospital bed inside his own familiar body.

After several comatose weeks, Arthur slowly re-emerged. The nurses and doctors closely monitored his condition. Arthur felt his strength returning. The nurses administered fluids. The doctors marveled at the speed of his recovery. Piercing above the mounting excitement, Arthur heard a feint yet distinct ringing. Arthur knew that ring. It was the harvester spirit's cell phone.

Seems there'd been a change of plans. The Happily Ever After Life Insurance Agency was officially back in business—its meaning and purpose now made clear. Somewhere little Ferdinand was just waking up, while Puma Wawa scratched her privates, shouted filthy, anti-man invective, and stirred her pancake batter. At long last, Arthur was going home.

Arthur: An Actuarial Odyssey

ABOUT THE AUTHOR

I have been a working sociologist since 1999. I have been a writer since 1976. And I have been a social satirist since 1970, after first boarding your planet in 1965. My fiction celebrates absurdist, social satire---an indispensable tool for exploring a world born of contradiction and driven by total faith in rationality and, above all, order.

I wrote my first book at age 11. It was a tell-all memoir. Lost long ago, under suspicious circumstances, the stories there told remain hidden to this day. My only aim today is to offer an occasional respite from the daily absurdities ailing all our actual lives. {And yes, should you Google my name [David Baronov], I am that guy, as well.)

But why then should you or anyone read my book? That is simple. A sociological perspective is the rarest viewpoint you will encounter today. Yet it is the only viable perspective for making sense of the lives we live and the world we experience.

Unfortunately, the ordinary venue for this perspective is nonfiction---a truly indigestible form. Thus, it is only fiction doused with the sociological that can truly capture the absurdity of our world and reimagine our reality. This explains the mission of Arthur: An Actuarial Odyssey.

Made in the USA
Monee, IL
18 October 2024